The
Jesus Women

the Jesus Women

MARCI ALBORGHETTI

TWENTY
THIRD *23rd*
PUBLICATIONS

Twenty percent of the royalties from *The Jesus Women* will be donated to the Mothers' Union Sierra Leone Pre-School Project in Freetown, Sierra Leone. The MU in the diocese of Freetown is working to rebuild an educational infrastructure that has been devastated by war and mismanagement.

Twenty-Third Publications
A Division of Bayard
One Montauk Avenue, Suite 200
PO Box 6015
New London, CT 06320
(860) 437-3012 or (800) 321-0411
www.23rdpublications.com
ISBN-10: 1-58595-576-0
ISBN 978-1-58595-576-3

The Scripture passages contained herein are from the *New Revised Standard Version of the Bible*, copyright ©1989, by the Division of Christian Education of the National Council of Churches in the U.S.A. All rights reserved.

Library of Congress Catalog Card Number: 2005936960
Printed in the U.S.A.

Dedication

For God.
To Charles.

Acknowledgments

I thank God for the inspirations that drive these stories and for my life. I am grateful to him for putting Gwen Costello, my publisher and editor at Twenty-Third Publications, in my path. Without her support and guidance my inspirations would have an extremely limited audience. I thank God for the priests, sisters, ministers, and other faithful servants who have taught me to bring my imagination to the study and worship of the Lord. The women in the New Testament—prophets, disciples, and friends of Jesus—offer examples of what strong, faithful women can become, and I am thankful for them. And finally, because we all know that behind every strong woman is a good man, I am thankful for Charlie.

Contents

Introduction

The women you will meet in these pages literally changed the face of history and religion. As contemporaries of Jesus Christ, they were in the extraordinary position to both witness and influence the development of the faith movement that transformed the world. They participated in a revolution that birthed a new religion. The first believers were determined to include the best things about Judaism, which ensured that Christians and Jews (like most families) would be forever engaged in a struggle that has both devastated and renewed the world. Today the Judeo-Christian world must acknowledge Islam, another world religion that also recognizes both Jesus and his Jewish mother, Mary. (In addition, all three religions claim Abraham as their patriarch and Moses as God's chosen leader.)

Women were there at the beginning, the genesis, of the Christian faith. They were there when Jesus confirmed and advanced the Judaic code of law that is the foundation for Christianity and much of civic law. They were there when Jesus performed the miracles and when he healed people, actions that continue to strengthen both individual and universal faith today. Women were there when he taught a religion of love and when he gave his life to prove the power of that love.

They were there. In this book, in narratives based on the gospels and on tradition, the women tell their stories in "their own words." As with *12 Strong Women of God*, which featured heroic women in the

Old Testament, this book offers first-person narratives of twelve women who experienced the life and times of Jesus. An Active Meditation and Reflection/Discussion Questions follow each story, which draws on information provided by the biblical writers, as well as by historians and commentators. The meditations and questions are useful for individual examination, for discussions, for study groups, and for book clubs.

CHAPTER 1

Mary

Mother and Prophet

LUKE 1:18—2:7

It seems strange to me that, with all that has happened, I still remember my girlhood so clearly. My life then was so simple, so easy. There were some in our village who thought I was spoiled, probably because I was my parents' only child. Though I was a daughter and not a son, my mother and father lavished attention on me. I was not spoiled, but I can understand why people thought I was. My mother and I were very close; more like sisters, some said. I was always amazed when I heard other girls talk about how stern their mothers were; it seemed that other mothers were constantly issuing orders and meting out punishments. "Do this, do that," the neighborhood girls would whine, imitating their own mothers. "If you don't start acting properly, you'll pay the price, girl!" Some girls would show marks from the beatings their mothers gave them. It was never this way between my mother and me.

I have no memory at all of her chastising me or disciplining me. Nor did she ever raise her voice to me, even later when I brought her the impossible news. She seemed content with me as I was, and we spent much time together at various chores, and I learned much earlier than other girls how to keep an efficient household and care for a flourishing garden that would provide food at little cost. Besides the usual cooking, sewing, and cleaning, my mother taught me how to carefully manage finances so that later I would be able to keep my family functioning with little money. Though most women did not teach their daughters such skills—they were thought to be the responsibility of men—my mother was fearless in this way.

She also taught me Scripture; my father feared she was going too far by teaching me. Girls never learned more than the rudimentary lessons from our books and written law, but my mother uncharacteristically opposed father in this. It was a gentle defiance, I admit, but she countered him all the same, insisting on teaching me the prophecies and deeper traditions of Israel.

My mother taught me Scripture during the day when my father was working, though not because she was afraid of him or wanted to deceive him. While she would not surrender something she believed was important, at the same time, she would not deliberately offend or aggravate my father. Or anyone, for that matter. When it came to my father and his opposition to our lessons, she felt no need to antagonize him. Thus she taught me strength and decency, independence and compassion. Later in life some people thought that I was quietly stubborn or even defiant, but the example my mother provided saw me through these difficulties. I think she must have somehow sensed what I would face. I came to understand that by doing this, she was teaching me how to conduct myself by providing herself as a model. Did she know? Did the Spirit guide her to this? I never asked her.

It was because of my mother and perhaps because of my own solitary nature that I never felt left out of the games and general silliness of my young neighbors and cousins. I never envied them their "normal childhood."

The one cousin I loved lived in the hill country of Judea, some distance from us. I seldom saw her. She was no playmate. Elizabeth was probably older than my mother, which suited me very well. I think I liked her better because of her age. She and mother were also great friends and our visits were full of laughter and comfort. The only sorrow was Elizabeth's childlessness. Although her husband Zechariah never reproached her for it, as many men would have, she felt it keenly. She never spoke of her childlessness in front of me, but it was in the air; there was heaviness amidst the mild perfume of contentment.

Once when I was very young, my mother and I went to spend a week with Elizabeth. I must have been about five years old. Zechariah was away at the temple, and it was just mother, Elizabeth, and I at dinner one evening. We had roasted goat, and I had trouble chewing the tough meat. My mother rose easily, as she would have at home, and bent over me to cut my food into small shreds. Her hair, thick and dark brown, brushed against my face. I reached up to take a soft curl in my small hand and press it gently against her cheek. At that moment my eyes fell on Elizabeth, gazing at us. Her lips were tightly pressed into a painful line, her eyes wide and round with the effort to hold in her anguish. There were no tears in them, just a raw, dry grief. My hand fell from my mother's face. I felt that I had done something inexplicably cruel. By the time mother finished with my food, Elizabeth had recovered and began chattering away merrily as though nothing had happened.

It was Elizabeth, not my mother, who told me about Joseph some years later during one of the rare visits my mother and I made to Elizabeth's distant house. My mother had gone to the market; she insisted on buying the food for dinner whenever we visited so we would not be an imposition on our cousin. "Mary, my child," Elizabeth began as we kneaded dough for the day's loaves, "you must be very excited! This Joseph is said to be a good man and a steady worker. And he was a wonderful husband to his wife before her early death. He has sons nearly your age. Although it's true that this sometimes that can be a problem—the first children can resent a young wife—you will win their love, child, with your goodness. Surely you will! Your mother thinks it's a good match. A carpenter! You will always have a dry, sturdy home and a good income!"

I was speechless, but since I was known for my reserve, Elizabeth did not notice. As she talked on of all the children I would bear, I tried to catch my breath. Why had my mother not told me? I knew that a man called Joseph visited my father a few times, but many men did business with father so I thought nothing of this. Well, that's not exactly true. Something had made me take special notice of this man. Not quite as old as father, he possessed a quiet self-assurance that drew my attention more compellingly than the younger, more handsome men did whose antics to impress me seemed foolish.

I knew Joseph had sons by a young wife whom he lost years before. Perhaps that's what made him seem so sober. Yet there was a steadiness and kindness to him that belied any hint of harshness. I sometimes watched from the walled garden when he called on father, observing his dignity and confidence. He was more attractive to me than the loud, arrogant young men in our area. Still, I never imagined that Joseph was interested in me.

Elizabeth's words were very unsettling. My feelings were confused. I was excited to learn of Joseph's interest—if it was even true and not my cousin's kind imaginings—but I was distressed that my mother had not told me. My mother and my father were not like some parents who all but sold their daughters to the highest bidders without even consulting them. No, my parents would never do such a thing. But why hadn't they told me that this man was seeking to marry me?

By the end of our visit with Elizabeth, I had all but convinced myself that Elizabeth had dreamed up this attachment. So on the journey home, my question to my mother was light-hearted and casual. "Our cousin has convinced herself that I am promised to the carpenter, Joseph, who does business with father! Whatever can have made her think so?"

I half-expected mother to laugh at Elizabeth's silly talk. When the silence between us lengthened, I turned to look into my mother's face. Her clear, olive skin had darkened, and she avoided my gaze. "Mother?"

When she looked at me, her eyes held a sort of plea, something I had never seen before. "He is a good man, Mary; a carpenter who would care deeply for you and keep you safe...." She would have gone on, but I interrupted her, "Yes, Elizabeth has already mentioned his considerable advantages, but why did I hear them first from her?" This response may seem cold, but my mother and I were accustomed to speaking easily and frankly with each other. And despite my respect and love for her, I was stunned and not a little frightened; I had thought my eventual marriage, though inevitable, was still at some safe distance.

My mother did not flinch from my words. "Mary," she said firmly, reestablishing the balance between us, "Your father is much older than I. And though I pray to God daily for his good health, life holds no certainties. Your father wants you safely settled with a good man before much more time passes. Joseph has much to recommend him. He lives nearby, so you would always be close to us. His sons are nearly grown. And besides, their mother's sister in Nazareth is raising them. They will not dominate your home. By all accounts, they will grow to be fine men and will make good brothers to your own children. Joseph's carpentry business is established; you will want for nothing. He is a kind man who was known to be very tender with his first wife. Indeed, she was very dependent on him. People say that he was the only one she trusted to help her in the births of their sons. My daughter, this fact is what won me over: I never heard of a man who loved his wife that much. Surely, I told myself, such a man will cherish and protect my beloved child. But, Mary, all you need to do is say no, and your father and I will never mention this again."

I did not say no. Joseph and I pledged ourselves to one another, and my father asked that I be allowed to remain at home for a year. I wasn't sure how to feel about this. As I came to know Joseph better, I grew eager to start my life as his wife. But I was also young enough to be relieved to have another year in the safety of my mother's house. I would go to sleep each night in my room, both wishing to join my husband and grateful to be in my own narrow bed.

It was into that room that the angel came. Gabriel, he named himself. When I first saw him, I was frightened. I had heard from my mother that an angel came upon Zechariah in the temple and had struck him mute. Was that what would happen to me? I cowered before the great light and heat surrounding the creature who was both magnificent and awful to look upon. I would have prostrated myself before him, but he spoke to prevent me. As though knowing the terror his appearance would cause me, he made his voice gentle.

Indeed, I did not hear him so much with my ears as in my heart and mind, a comforting language within me.

When I look back upon those moments and at what Gabriel told me, I wonder at my reaction. Why wasn't I terrified, ready to flee in fear from such an announcement? Why did I not dissolve into frantic tears and beg to be released from this incomprehensible burden? Where did I find the courage to protest my virginity? How did I speak the words of humble consent rather than cry out for my mother?

Many years would pass before I really understood my reaction to Gabriel's impossible message. My heart slowed as he spoke, and I experienced an unlikely serenity. My mind, astonishingly, began to grasp the magnitude of his words. I recalled the Scripture my mother had taught me about a prophecy concerning a Messiah.

What concerns I had were not for myself, unlikely as that may seem. My concerns were for my parents, my family, and my neighbors, what they would think and say. Yet even those worries, the concerns of a dutiful daughter, dissipated in the soft, deep echo of Gabriel's tone. When he left, the peace that had filled me stayed with me. My one sorrowful thought was, "Joseph, I will lose Joseph."

How could Joseph ever take me into his home as his wife now? How could he face his neighbors, his friends, and especially his sons? He would be an object of laughter, a husband thought to be betrayed before he had the chance to take his wife to his bed. He would be shamed. I couldn't bear to think of how his gentle face would look when he learned that I carried a child. I couldn't bear to think of how it would hurt him.

My mother was thinking of other things. "He could have you stoned," she said in a low, agonized voice when I told her of the angel and the child within me. As frightened as I was by her reaction, somewhere inside me I felt a sense of relief—even joy, if that is possible—that she never doubted my word, never once questioned my story of Gabriel's visit or of the origin of my child. Instead, she worried about what would happen to me if Joseph sought the full measure of punishment.

I tried to comfort her. "Mother, he wouldn't do that! He is too good a man. He is not a hot-tempered young husband bent on revenge to soothe his fury. He has no cruelty in him and no thirst for punishment. I only mourn how this will hurt and embarrass him."

My mother said no more. I don't think she was convinced of Joseph's temperance because she soon packed me off to spend several months with Elizabeth, away from our village and the prying eyes of neighbors and, more important, away from Joseph and his family. Elizabeth herself was miraculously pregnant, and I would be of use to her, my mother said. I made no argument. Though the peace within me held strong, I was very aware of the pain and confusion I caused those I loved. My mother insisted that I go to Elizabeth's without telling Joseph. She said that my father would speak to him after I was safely with my cousin.

The journey was easy, even though I was in the early stage of pregnancy; I never became sick as so many women do in those first months.

My stay with Elizabeth was satisfying and joyful. As soon as she caught sight of me, instead of embracing me as her young cousin, she greeted me as if unable to stop herself: "Blessed are you among women, and blessed is the fruit of your womb. And why has this happened to me, that the mother of my Lord comes to me? For as soon as I heard the sound of your greeting, the child in my womb leapt for joy."

Her greeting, and my response, revealed much about God's plan for me and for future generations. "My soul magnifies the Lord, and my spirit rejoices in God my Savior, for he has looked with favor on the lowliness of his servant. Surely, from now on all generations will call me blessed; for the Mighty One has done great things for me, and holy is his name. His mercy is for those who fear him from generation to generation. He has shown strength with his arm; he has scattered the proud in the thoughts of their hearts. He has brought down the powerful from their thrones, and lifted up the lowly; he has filled the hungry with good things, and sent the rich away empty. He has helped his servant Israel, in remembrance of his mercy, according to the promise he made to our ancestors, to Abraham and to his descendants forever."

That wondrous discourse between Elizabeth and me, and between the sons in us, made it suddenly clear to me how utterly life had changed. I was exhausted when I finished speaking. Elizabeth had to bear me into my room, where I slept deeply until the next morning.

The next three months were idyllic, as though this Spirit-driven exchange had been just a dream. Elizabeth and I found as much pleasure in each other's company as we always had. I helped her more and more with her daily tasks, as she grew large. The portent of our words remained silently in my mind. Perhaps I cherished this simple time all the more because I knew it would soon end.

By the time I returned to my parents' house, my father had told Joseph about my child. This was fortunate because it was clear to all by then that I was pregnant. There were many curious, knowing, and even hostile stares as I came into our village, and I was hurried inside our house. As I predicted, Joseph had no intention of either having me stoned or publicly accusing me of adultery. Not that any public accusation would be needed, if the glances of my neighbors were any measure. I could not bring myself to ask how Joseph had responded to the news. My mother told me, "Joseph has decided that he will end the marriage quietly, put you away as a wife and send you back to our home as our daughter. It is the kindest possible judgment he could make."

Though I could tell she was relieved for my sake, I could not help but feel sad. I felt I had hurt Joseph. I knew he must be embarrassed, if not humiliated, at the whisperings that surely followed him. They would call him foolish for pledging himself to an unfaithful girl. No one would know the truth, and if they knew it, few would believe it. My heart wept for Joseph and I suppose, a little for myself.

Yet the peace in my heart persisted through this trial. An aura of calm surrounded me, radiating outward and protecting me from all that was happening. As my son grew in me, I began to feel that we were isolated, that the world bustled around us but could not truly touch us. I felt no need to think beyond the moment; I knew we would be taken care of.

One day my solitude was interrupted when my mother brought me news that Joseph was waiting for me in the garden. My breath caught in my throat for a moment. He must have come to express his disappointment or even anger, and I knew he was justified. I took a deep breath and went out to meet him.

I was surprised at the calm expression on his face. There was no anger or even sadness. He strode over to me and grasped my hands. "Mary"—he breathed out my name as if it was something he held inside for a long time—"I've had a dream, a dream that affirms all that you said, that the child in you is from God."

I smiled in delight. "So you came to forgive me?"

"No! It is you who must forgive me! For the angel in my dream told me that I am to take you as my wife and to cherish you and your son. I am to keep and protect you both as best I can. Mary, will you still have me as your husband?"

He had never ceased to be my husband in God's eyes, and I told him so. He took me that very day into his home, and within a short time we had the news of the Roman census. Joseph and I would have to travel to Bethlehem to be counted. He was worried about the trip, for I was close to my time. He wondered if we should go at all, if it wouldn't be safer to defy the Romans. But when I reminded him of his dream and that we were in now God's hands, he nodded in his stoic way and began to pack our belongings.

The sense of placid well-being that God had given me faltered only once in all this time. I wept when I took leave of my mother. Though I could not say what the future held, I somehow knew I might not see her again. My mother, my teacher, my sister, and companion! She who endured sorrow and disdain on my behalf, she who held her head high while others whispered and gossiped about her "precious daughter." She had been the center of my life until Gabriel came to me. Next to the child who was now a part of me, I had never loved anyone so completely. And yet it was I who finally pulled away from our parting embrace and allowed my husband to lift me onto the foal that would carry me to Bethlehem. Every time I looked back, my mother was standing where I left her, until finally the distance made her vanish. How long did she remain there, watching, even after I had disappeared?

I often considered these events, once all that concerned my Son and myself was fulfilled. I came to believe only one explanation for my life and the peace I felt. When the Father gave his Son to my body, he must also have given his Spirit to my soul. The courage I found, my consent, the impossible calm that filled me at Gabriel's words, even the glorious prophecy I uttered in response to Elizabeth's miraculous greeting—all these were from God. And when my time came and his Son left my body, God's Spirit stayed with me. Through everything I was to face, the Spirit was my strength, my only comfort. I nearly relinquished the Spirit when I watched my Son writhe and groan on the cross, but in the end, I clung to the Spirit despite my unspeakable anguish. Even then, God was with me. Even then. Even now.

Active Meditation

Because Mary courageously said yes to God, God was able to work through her. Take her as your model. Are you prevented by fear from speaking a truth or taking action you believe you should take? Perhaps you want to speak or write about your faith, to confront your child about destructive behavior, to address a troubling issue in your marriage, or to fight an injustice in your community. Do you fear ridicule, embarrassment, or shame? Mary called upon the Spirit to preserve her as both prophet and mother. Call upon that same Spirit as you proclaim the truth or take action. Welcome the Spirit into your being just as Mary did and remain secure in the presence of God, regardless of the opinions of others.

Reflection/Discussion Questions

1. When have you felt God calling or leading you? Describe the situation. How did God's call change your life?

2. Mary was supported by her mother, her cousin, and her husband, all moved by the Holy Spirit. In what ways do you feel supported by close family members or your spouse? Do you see the Holy Spirit working in these relationships?

3. Describe a situation when you were tempted to judge a person because of appearances, only to learn later that your judgment would have been in error. What amends do you think can be made when someone is gossiped about and the person's reputation is harmed?

CHAPTER II

Anna

A Life of Faith Affirmed

LUKE 2:22–38

Every day in the temple I raise my voice in prophecy and praise of the Lord. At night in my bed, I silently pray for him to take me. How much longer must I remain here, trapped in this world of misery, proclaiming the hope of a Messiah many of my people no longer believe will come? When will the Father draw me to him and give me peace? I have announced his word for years. Is it not enough that I watched Romans overrun our nation and encircle our temple with their pagan soldiers? Is it not enough that I must see our leaders cringe before the occupying force, trading tradition for security? Jerusalem is under siege, and I yearn to be taken from this place where I am no longer heard.

Only memories offer a reprieve to my burdened heart. When I close my eyes, I see him as though the many years that have passed are nothing. My husband. My love. The only man I ever wanted. Even after all this time, I can hardly convince myself that our time together was so brief. In the span of years, seven is nothing, and yet I lived a lifetime in those seven years. We were married when I was eighteen;

my parents were worried that they would never marry me off. It was not for lack of offers that I remained unmarried. I had many proposals. My father was wealthy enough to provide a generous dowry, and I was beautiful in those days. Now I am a crone. My skin is wrinkled and burned by the wind and sun, my hands are gnarled and cramped, and I am clothed in clean rags and worn sandals. There is only a vestige of my former self that remains in my face or body.

Before I was married, the men lined up outside our door, according to my mother anyway. She did not mean this necessarily as a compliment. She talked about the men to chastise me because I would have none of them. I was as proud as I was lovely, my skin pale and tinted with roses, my raiment soft and beautiful, my sandals of the finest dyed leather, my hair lustrous and dressed with jewels. I could not be moved to take a man not of my choosing. In her frustration my mother would remonstrate, "What is wrong with you? The men wait in a line, and yet you are too good for any of them! How can it be that a daughter of mine should be so obstinate and cold-hearted? Have you no feeling for your father and me, for the whispers we must endure over your improper refusals and disobedience?"

I did feel a pang for the distress I caused them. I deeply loved my father, Phanuel. We were of the tribe of Asher, and I knew well that many expected my father to make a good marriage for me, a task I was making nigh impossible for him. But I did not feel enough remorse to change my ways. I insisted that I should be able to choose the man I would have to spend my life with, but that was not the real (at least not the only) reason I withstood so many advances. The truth was that I did not wish to marry at all and had no intention of doing so. Whether my mother suspected this or not, I cannot say, but it would not surprise me. She was nearly beside herself with me, but I was my father's only beloved and indulged (it's true) daughter. I knew he would not force me. Thus mother had no recourse and was reduced to bitter mutterings. I hoped to stall until it was too late, until no man would want me.

As strange as it may seem, it was my love of Scripture that kept me from wanting to marry. My father had given me leave to study as much as I wished, one more thing my mother objected to, and I read all the books of Israel by the time I was twelve years old. I was more fascinated by the people than by the myriad rules and laws. The ancient Hebrew women and prophets particularly thrilled me, and I vowed to model myself after them. They would be my true forebears.

I would be a judge like Deborah, a warrior like Judith, a queen like Esther…though I intended to fulfill that particular role without consorting with a king. After all, he would just get in the way. Didn't these women rise far above the men who surrounded them, surpassing them in wisdom, courage, and wit? I needed no husband to become a Jewish heroine; my readings taught me that much. I longed to shoulder the burdens of my people, to lead them back to the place they so richly deserved. I longed to be God's messenger on earth, wise and just. And most of all, unmarried.

Of course I dared not tell anyone of my intentions, dreams they were, I know now. But at that time I was determined to reject all suitors. With each rejection my father was worn down a bit more, even as my mother grew more sternly determined that I should marry. By the time I reached the nearly scandalous age of seventeen, I could see that the battle for my father's will would be between my mother and me. To this day I cannot say who might have won, had my husband not decided the issue.

My future husband was passing through our village with no intention of finding himself a wife. Truly, I sometimes wonder if he was as determined as I was not to marry. A peddler by appearance, there was nothing about him to suggest the impressive store of wealth he already inherited from his father in Jerusalem. And a good thing, too, because I would have never given him a second thought if he dressed and acted the role of respectable merchant. Like me, though, he was not what he seemed. Although he did not neglect selling wares to the villagers, he was eager to engage in discourse about the law and our traditions. He was welcomed into the many discussions of the Scripture during the time he lodged with one of the villagers. Though women did not attend these gatherings, my father went frequently. It was my father who spoke to my mother and me about this traveling merchant, whom my father called "both brilliant and disturbing in his speech."

Well, that was all I needed to hear. Suddenly the dusty peddler took on new interest for me. Watching him whenever I could, I noticed that he was not handsome in any ordinary way, a positive point from my perspective since I had long grown disgusted with my so-called handsome suitors. These suitors were all too aware of their physical advantages and expected me to be overwhelmed with their beauty. No, this man was unusual to look upon. "Ugly," my mother dismissed him in a disdainful tone. She did not know, of course, about the fine home with its full coffers he built for himself in Jerusalem. But I thought of him as interesting rather than ugly with his long, gaunt body, tangled black hair, and rough, sun-bronzed skin. Most interesting were his eyes. I expected them to be dark, but found them to be a clear, sea green on that morning when he finally turned them full upon me.

That day I felt myself flush with embarrassment as he regarded me frankly. I thought I was observing him surreptitiously, but what did I know of such things at seventeen? He turned swiftly, catching me watching him. After a long, excruciating moment of staring at me, he asked, "Why do you follow me? Do you wish to buy something for your mother?"

It's impossible to name all the emotions that rushed through me at his words: searing shame that he caught me watching him, fear that he would think me immodest, and fury that he dismissed me as a child with nothing better to do than to run errands for my mother. But another emotion overrode them all. He mesmerized me, his eyes boring through me as if searching for something vital. For the first time in my life, I couldn't speak.

Fortunately for me (although I didn't know it at that moment), he was as taken with me as I with him. Much later he told me, "I couldn't move. I didn't know what to say. The only thing I could think of was that I had to keep you from walking away before I discovered who you were."

In the end, he broke the silence. "What is your name, then?"

"Anna." I murmured, recovering enough to add, "Your speech has made an impression on my father, Phanuel."

His eyes lit with amused recognition. "Ah yes. I know Phanuel, but I fear the impression I left is not all good."

"That's not true!" I responded quickly and not entirely truthfully. "He calls you 'brilliant.'"

"And what else does he call me?" he asked, with the wide grin that won me completely.

I looked down, blushing more furiously, but he had pity on me and said seriously, "The village men say that Phanuel errs in teaching his only daughter Scripture. Is this true?"

"Not that he errs," I said boldly, "but that he teaches me, yes."

He looked at me for a long time before asking, "And how well has he taught you? What do you know?"

And from that moment on, we never stopped talking. How could I resist someone who knew so much, and who believed it was right for his wife to be as educated as he was? All my feelings about marriage changed. We talked of Deborah, Judith, and Esther. And then we talked of Moses, David, Isaiah, Susannah, Daniel, and Abraham. And then we talked of Isaac, Ismael, and Sarah.

The conversation and the love that was born that day flourished until my young husband died nearly eight years later. I have never looked at another man since, nor I have been tempted to look. Something simply died when my husband died. I could not love another if I wanted to.

There are few true men left in Israel, for how could they sustain their manhood in the face of so much violence, so many failed uprisings, a Roman occupation, and the false prophets? How are they to be men when they no longer know how? There are no men like my husband with the courage to call on God and to truly know his books. There is no Messiah, no prophets, to teach them.

And so my dream, though it has become a nightmare, has come true: I am Deborah, but no one attends to my judgment or my prophecies. I am Judith, but no enemy lets me come close enough to save my people. I am Esther, but there is no king to match my courage and no saving edict to issue. My people are under attack, adrift, cut loose from their strength, waiting for their God, and wondering if God has forgotten them. Can they hope for a Messiah when a creature like Herod calls himself our king? Can there be a prophet in Israel when Caesar demands a census and our people scurry to obey like sheep following the wolf? Can there be hope when the brutish, armor Roman soldiers patrol our city gates and lay siege to our temple?

I am ready to be taken from my people. I have done what I could, and it is not enough. I praise God every day, prophesying about the Messiah who will surely come; yet my voice is unheeded. I remind the people of God's promise, but they grow nearer to despair with every false uprising, and some begin to prefer violence to faith. Yet despite my prayers, God has not taken me. Despite my great age and greater sorrow, I am still here in this temple, speaking daily words of hope that fall on deaf ears.

I find myself wondering if God has a reason for keeping me here. Even as I think myself depleted, useless, I consider that God may have a different thought, for there is something that has captured my interest. Strange tidings have reached even my ancient ears, news of events unimagined. There has been talk of kings from the east who traveled endless miles to see a baby they call a king. I myself, even I with my clouded eyes, saw the star they are said to have followed to the child's birthplace. Bethlehem, just as the prophecies foretold. There are rumors that the child himself was born of a miracle, and that the mother is hardly more than a child herself. It is whispered that she is a virgin, even after giving birth.

The temple hums quietly, excitedly, with such news and with the most recent word that Herod is frantic at these murmurings. They say he never sleeps now, pacing and calling for his learned men to interpret Scripture about the birth of the Messiah. His mad, blood-veined eyes are turned fearfully toward Bethlehem. He knows the kings went there, but did not return to him. My friend Simeon, a good and holy man who himself awaits the coming of the Messiah, told me that the kings deliberately thwarted Herod. They refused to tell him where they found the child, and they returned to their land by secret routes.

Simeon speaks of a horror. There are whispers that Herod, frustrated by the wise men and maddened by the word that a king has been born, plans to murder all male infants in the region where the child was born. Herod hopes to ensure that the new king will die before he can threaten Herod's throne. Simeon cannot believe such a thing, even of Herod, but I am not surprised. He is a sick and twisted old man, his life and heritage slipping from him by the moment. He would do any-thing, even mimick the Egyptians who so long ago murdered our first-born sons. It is said that his son, Herod Antipas, is worse.

I slept poorly last night after considering all these things, and I am anxious to meet with Simeon today to discuss them and hear any news he might have. I move slowly these days, and my joints ache continuously. As I make my way to the temple proper, a few stop and greet me respectfully but most stay out of my way. I have made few friends with my persistent prophesying. There are few men who can tolerate a female prophet in any event. They have forgotten the women of the Torah, my women, those who ruled and judged Israel. Would that such a woman arise today.

The woman before me, standing by Simeon, is just a child herself. Slender and small, she does not bear the look of a prophet, and yet something about her arrests my halting steps. I find myself frozen several paces away from them, observing the scene before me with growing awe. Standing between Simeon and a man who must be her husband, the woman holds an infant carefully dressed in clean swad-dling clothes. And now I notice that the woman, though slight, is far from fragile. There is a suppleness about her, a suggestion of the wil-low that will bend but not break. Her face is unusually calm; there is none of the anxiety of a new mother at such an important ceremony. Indeed, though very young, her eyes are already ancient, speaking an untold wisdom. The sight of her unsettles me.

The father has with him the tokens of purification for a son. In small cages he bears two turtledoves, and I know they are presenting their first-born. He is an older man, strong looking, and he is con-versing with Simeon while the mother remains silent, her whole attention on the child in her arms. It is as if she wishes to memorize everything about him.

As do I. It is not this tableau of a young family presenting their first-born child, typical in the temple, that has captured me. It is the child. It is not just how the mother cradles him as though bearing something precious beyond measure, although that is how she holds him. It is not just that the child, unlike most infants who squall through their presentation, is wholly silent, although he is. It is not just how he nestles in his mother's arm, peaceful and motionless, although such stillness in a waking infant is unusual.

It is that the child is watching. His eyes, fathomless and dark in his flawless face, are on all around him. This child drinks in everything around him, quietly, as if he knows what he sees. His face is solemn, full of comprehension, and there is a light in his eyes that seems to clear and sharpen my own dull sight. I feel as though he is united not only with his parents, but also with all people who are in the temple and indeed, with the temple itself.

Just as I was all those years ago when I first met my husband, I am now mesmerized and filled with a love that surpasses even that human bond. This, I know, is the child of Bethlehem.

Simeon takes the infant in his arms and begins to praise God for letting him see this child, the salvation of Israel. But Simeon's words fade as my ears are filled with a beloved tone.

"Anna," my husband's voice breathes into my heart, "here is the One! The One we waited for and talked about and prayed for. The One who kept us up nights talking. The One for whom your heroines preserved Israel. And now, my love, my wife, my prophet...speak!"

When his words are stilled, the words of Isaiah move through my soul:

> For a child has been born for us, a son given to us; authority rests upon his shoulders; and he is named Wonderful Counselor, Mighty God, Everlasting Father, Prince of Peace. His authority shall grow continually, and there shall be endless peace for the throne of David and his kingdom. He will establish and uphold it with justice and with righteousness from this time onward and forevermore.
>
> A shoot shall come out from the stump of Jesse, and a branch shall grow out of his roots. The spirit of the Lord shall rest on him, the spirit of wisdom and understanding, the spirit of counsel and might, the spirit of knowledge and the fear of the Lord.

And moving forward toward the mother and her child, I straighten my bony shoulders, raise my crippled hands and speak.

Active Meditation

Do you ever wonder if God is listening to you? You are not alone. Even people of great faith sometimes feel abandoned by God. Biblical examples include Esther, Job, Jonah, David, Jeremiah, Isaiah, Peter, Thomas, Matthew, Paul, and, of course, Anna. Many of the saints struggled with their faith, including modern-day "saints," such as Dorothy Day, Bishop Oscar Romero, and Mother Teresa. Try to learn more about a saint and how God led this person to faith. Take note of how God remained faithful, even when the person's faith flagged or faltered. Today, as in Anna's day, it is not easy to sustain and articulate faith. If we have faith like Anna's, we will find the courage to persist.

Reflection/Discussion Questions

1. Have you ever felt that God is calling you to express your faith more openly? How, if at all, did you respond to this call?

2. Who has been a person of faith in your life? How did you accept his or her message?

3. Anna's times are similar to our own, anxious and uncertain. She preached the coming of the Messiah. How do you "preach" the message that Jesus has come and dwells among us?

CHAPTER III

The Widow of Nain

Grief Transformed

LUKE 7:11–17

I know all these people who have gathered in this procession to help me mourn my son, and yet none among them can imagine what I feel. They think they can know what I feel. I know they mean well, but who among them can truly comprehend my grief? My grief upon grief upon grief. My son was all I had. Now he is borne on the bier of death as we follow the procession out of our city.

When my husband died so young, my grief was for my love and my youth. It is a grief that many women of Israel must know, that women all over the world know. It is grief that we must bear. And so I did. I mourned for all I lost, but I rejoiced for all we had together. Most especially, I rejoiced in our son, our only child. I was left to raise him on my own, but I saw his father live on in him. Some days it was as if his father was still with us, they were that much alike. In that, I found the strength to go on, and later, I even found joy. He was the symbol of our love even as he grew into a man in his own right.

My son had enough years with his father to both remember and honor him, and I admit that this made me proud. Was I too proud?

But what profit is there in considering such things now? My boy was like his father in many ways, in his quiet way of holding his head a little to the side when he listened, the careful, courteous way he ate, and the way he helped me clean and separate the eating and cooking vessels. He loved our old city, Nain, even when he could have moved to a larger, more prosperous place like Jerusalem. My son had an affinity for the land and was skilled at nurturing our small garden, despite the poor soil and lack of rain, just like his father. And like his father he was willing to work hard and save what he earned to ensure our comfort. In that, he was most like his father, always anxious that I should be secure with no worries about money. My husband also worried about this, though I would try to dismiss his concerns.

"I have no fear that you will provide for me well into my old age." I would laugh, trying to lighten his mood.

"Do not make light of this, wife; my father died young and his father before him. What if I cannot be with you in your old age?" he would ask soberly. When I would turn away, unable to bring myself to answer him, he would try to reassure me. "At least I can be sure that you will never want for anything."

As if any amount of money could have made up for his absence. As it was, he died before he could completely secure the future for my son and me (although there was enough put by to keep us from hunger until my son could work). And the child, like his father, was determined to take a trade and work to remove from my shoulders the burden of supporting us. I never wanted him to work as hard as he did, apprenticed at the age of fifteen to a skilled tent-maker, but he insisted. For the next seventeen years, he worked every day except Sabbaths and feast days. By the time he was twenty-two, he had his own business; his work was prized all over the region. Some of the best families in Israel came to him, but he was not proud.

I kept telling him it was time for him to marry, start a family. "Where are my grandchildren?" I would joke with him, but we both knew I was half-serious. He was my only child, and as much comfort as he gave me, I wanted him to have sons to carry on his father's name. I did not want my husband's name and memory to die out in Israel. But my son was not ready to marry.

"Mother," he would reply to my teasing, "there's plenty of time for that. My business is prosperous and I want to save enough for you and the family I will someday have to live well. Be patient!"

So I was. And truly, it was easy to be patient with him, for he was such a joy to me. We took our evening meal together, often joining neighbors for the Sabbath celebration and festivals. Our small vegetable garden was renowned in Nain, and we often brought a portion of our bounty to our hosts. We attended every wedding and rejoiced with every family, just as we participated in every funeral procession and offered what comfort we could. All of Nain was our family. My son was no scholar, but he was devoted to the law and lived according to the commandments given to Moses.

He was scrupulous about our laws of washing and purification, though like his father, he was never one to study Scripture or engage in the endless discussions of our rabbis and learned men. He preferred to work the land or make tents. Our life was simple but full, and he was never far from me. He spent his days in the workshop he built near our house. On the rare occasions he traveled to Jerusalem for work, I missed him a great deal. But I always consoled myself with the thought that, in the end, I would not be alone. Surely it would be he and his wife and sons who would bury me. That is the right and natural way of things. How can an aging mother imagine burying her strong, young son?

It was last year on one of his infrequent trips to Jerusalem that he met Micala. She was the only daughter of a wealthy Pharisee who hired my son. It was the first time he ever delayed returning home from a work project. I knew that he met someone as soon as he sent me word that he would be late. And knowing my son, I knew that whoever could keep him from his home and shop would surely be the one he married. I was ready for his news when he finally returned, nearly a week past his expected time.

"Mother," he began, his face flushed and his eyes bright.

"Tell me all about her, my child," I interrupted him, smiling a little. The look on his face was precious to me. He was astonished that I knew, as if I had not long ago learned to read every sign on his face, every decision in his mind. Blushing, he quickly recovered himself.

In the time it took for his face to lose the expression he had worn as a five year old when he thought I knew everything, I realized that I was about to lose my son to another woman.

And it was time. I told myself that as he described Micala. Never was a woman made who was more beautiful. No sweeter of disposition. She was the living symbol of grace and kindness. Faithful to the law, as the daughter of a leading Pharisee, she had been taught all the proper traditions of our people and was as pious as any daughter of Israel could be. As my son talked on, I began to fear he lost his sense just a little, but then he reassured me of his sanity, adding, "And, Mother, she is the well-loved daughter of a very wealthy father. There will be a substantial dowry along with an annual allowance once our children begin to come. I need not worry about supporting our family, and the money we have saved together will be yours always. As father would have wished."

I suppressed a small smile. It seemed my son had found the ideal woman...for both his heart and his purse. Still I could not help but feel touched that he remained solicitous of his father and me, even in the first flush of love. And I knew that he did, indeed, love this girl, for no amount of dowry could have moved him this way. He talked of her during our evening meal and long into the night.

We talked of his plans to build a new home for his wife and family on our property. He explained, "You must still have your privacy, Mother, but we will be close by should you need us. And you will know your grandchildren." The cost of the house would deplete our savings, but the dowry would replace it. He knew he would earn the money back in a short time, particularly given the new work he would likely obtain from his father-in-law's many wealthy colleagues.

Like any mother, especially a widowed mother who was so close to her son and so dependent on him, I was anxious about meeting my future daughter-in-law. My son's glowing description of her did nothing to allay my worries: what aging mother would be eager to meet such a paragon of Hebrew womanhood? It was hard not to whisper to myself that with so much beauty and so many advantages, she must also be spoiled and demanding. Perhaps his loving eyes did not see it, but I feared mine certainly would.

I could not have been more mistaken. My son had not exaggerated Micala's virtues. She agreed to make the journey from Jerusalem to Nain just to meet me. Although she would move to our home some months before the actual wedding, this trip to meet me was a courtesy and kindness, and I was deeply conscious of it on the morning she was to arrive. I wondered if she resented me already for having to leave the comfort of her father's luxurious home in Jerusalem for the jolting, dusty journey to Nain, where the major social event was the women's daily procurement of water at the nearest well. Why would she want to trade lounging in her father's meticulously tended, walled gardens with their lovely olive and pomegranate trees for working in the dirt in our struggling, little vegetable patch? How would a child of such prosperity and status fare in this small, unremarkable city? By the time she arrived, I convinced myself that I should try to dissuade my son from moving his wife to Nain. I would sacrifice our closeness to help preserve his marriage and prevent his wife from a moldering, bitter boredom.

Within minutes of meeting Micala, all my fears had fled. At nineteen years old, she was much younger than my son but still older than most brides. I could see immediately why her parents must have been happy to keep her with them for as long as they could. She approached me gently, walking softly on her toes, her eyes downcast and her hands held out in an imploring sort of gesture. Despite what must have been an uncomfortable journey, she was as fresh as a blooming vine, yet she could hardly bring herself to turn her fine, dark eyes upon my face. Her voice, though sweet and deep, was so low that I could barely hear her murmured greeting.

At first I did not know what to make of this unexpected impression. But as I studied her high, smooth forehead and small, straight nose above well-shaped lips, I realized that though her beauty was riveting, she was shy, perhaps painfully so. I understood that it was the combination of her loveliness and this appealing natural reticence that had attracted my son. This was a woman he could both care for and take care of, and I knew he would find this desirable. I wondered briefly, as I led her into our home, whether she would be a strong enough wife for him, but I forced myself to dismiss this as a small concern compared to my relief at finding her so appealing. After all, the girl had never been away from her parents, and I should not expect her to be bold or even confident in such a discomfiting situation. I imagined she must miss her mother terribly.

She stayed with us that first time through the Sabbath, and as the days passed, her natural warmth shone through her reserve. Though my son spent as much time as he could with her, he had to complete the work her father had commissioned before he brought her back to Jerusalem. Once I became used to her quiet demeanor, Micala became a good companion, naturally taking upon herself certain chores and responsibilities. At first I resisted her efforts to help in the house and garden. I soon understood, however, that this was her way of showing that she was growing more accustomed to me. When I first protested her working so hard during the visit, she said softly, "I want to learn what I should do to make a good home for us." What more could I ask for?

Beyond that, she said little, but I realized that this was not a failing of hers so much as an expression of comfort. And I am sure I spoke enough for both of us. She was not much more talkative in my son's presence, but there was a glow about her when he came in for the evening that warmed my heart and awoke the memories of how I felt when first married to his father. We did not speak so much during our first year together either, but I never remember feeling oppressed or lonely. Quite the opposite. Micala would do well by my son, and he, I knew, by her.

By the time my son was ready to bring her back to her parents, I was convinced that all would be well and looked forward to her return in several months to live with me after they were formally betrothed. One thing only concerned me. I was left with the notion that I was wrong about the closeness between Micala and her parents. I knew she had been clearly raised in the tradition of Israel and with all the outward advantages of a wealthy daughter, but I sensed there was little warm feeling between her and her parents.

It was not that she said anything to convey this impression. But whenever I mentioned her mother, she became even quieter and did not reply, except as courtesy required. Once when she dropped a jar

of water and it shattered, she became so pale and trembled so violently, I did not know how to comfort her. Her eyes were wildly fearful and searching mine as though expecting me to shriek at her or
slap her. Surprised, I murmured quiet words of comfort, "It is nothing, child. Just an old vase! And we are not so far from the well that
we will be at a loss by an extra trip if we need more water." As I wondered about whether to gently embrace her, she threw on her cloak
and, taking up an empty jar, hurried out to the well for more water.
I called after her that it was not necessary but she paid me no heed.
When she returned some time later, she seemed much more com-
posed and did not speak of the accident that had been so slight in
my mind but so large in hers.

I decided to say no more, but I began to wonder. She took such
evident pleasure in just being close to me, performing everyday tasks,
almost as if she was learning what it was like to be a daughter. There
was something both innocent and watchful about her. She was like
a child unschooled in the normal ways of life, but too familiar with
its more frightening aspects. And though she relaxed as the brief days
passed, her manner became anxious and uncertain as the hour she
was to return came upon us. My son did not notice, or if he did, gave
no sign of it. We rose at dawn on the day she was to leave, and she
could not eat the hot milled grain with a little honey and goat's milk
I prepared for breakfast. When my son called in to her that he was
ready, she began to shuffle toward the door, and then she astonished
me by turning back and throwing herself into my open arms. I held
her for a long while. She did not cry or make a sound but she trembled violently. When my son finally came in to see what delayed her,
she broke away abruptly, as though not wanting him to see her dis-
play of emotion. After mumbling a quiet farewell, she was gone.

I was never to see her again.

When my son returned home from delivering her and the newly-
made tents to her parents, I told him what I observed and asked him
directly about her parents. It had always been our habit, particularly
since my husband died, to speak openly with each other. I knew
from my neighbors that it was not often thus between mother and
son, but we had always been close and did not hesitate to speak

clearly. My son seemed uncertain as to how to respond, and I realized that he did not wish to speak ill of his future in-laws. But as was our custom, he answered honestly.

"I cannot say just what the problem is. They are courteous to me, but in truth, her father treats me no differently now than when I was merely his tent-maker. He was polite and businesslike then, as he is now, but there is no warmth there, no welcome. I have spent even less time in the mother's presence, but she is, if anything, colder." He hesitated and glanced at me before continuing. "You know how I dislike gossip. But the household's chief steward, who took a liking to me when I introduced him to a wine merchant who sold a favored vintage at a good price, speaks freely to me. At times, I wonder if he isn't warning me. He said that Micala is almost a prisoner in that house and that her father has never forgiven his wife for not giving him a son, something vital for a Pharisee. The wife, in turn, has taken her husband's bitterness out on Micala.

"Who can say if any of this is true? The chief steward has no great love for his master, who seems to deal harshly with the household servants. Still, I have seen no real affection between the husband and wife, and certainly none shown toward Micala. The steward told me that for once, the girl stood up for herself and told her parents that she wants me. I asked him if they had at first opposed my suit, and he became silent and dismayed. When I persisted, he admitted that they had forbidden her to encourage me, refusing to let her marry a tradesman. They told her that I knew nothing of Scripture and seldom visited the synagogue, much less engaged in debate with the learned men. They could not let their daughter marry such a man. Micala threatened to kill herself and bring shame upon them all. She assured them that the servants would spread her story through all of Jerusalem and that, one way or another, she would be free, and they would be humiliated. So her parents agreed and provided a large dowry to keep people from talking. I think the sooner I bring her home here, the better."

My son finished, looking as disturbed as I felt. Indeed, I was horrified, as much at the dire situation Micala was now in as at the malicious attitude of her parents toward my son. There was no better man in Israel. I was both indignant for my family and frightened for the girl. I tried to comfort my son and urged him to start building their new dwelling. The sooner we could send for the girl the better. I worried for her fragile state of mind; the threat to take her own life distressed me greatly. Though they would not come together until after the wedding, at least she could live out the betrothal under her own roof where I could stay with her while my son in our old home. Since there was nothing to object to in such a familiar and respectable arrangement, I imagined her parents would now wish to be rid of her as soon as appearances would allow.

My son began to work impossibly long days, using the daylight to work on his commissions and the dawn and twilight hours on the new house. I am ashamed now to say that I encouraged him in this, ever mindful of that poor girl in Jerusalem. And besides, I missed her company.

During these weeks, my son and I had only one diversion. Talk had reached Nain about the traveling preacher called Jesus, the Christ. Many in our village could talk of nothing else. Some said that Jesus was a gifted teacher, some, the Messiah. Others, like my son's future father-in-law, a Pharisee who commanded the respect of many, believed he was a dangerous revolutionary. Perhaps this is why my son became so interested in Jesus. My son believed the wonderful things being said about Jesus.

And though my boy had never been one to study Scripture, he became a vocal advocate of Jesus in Nain. I worried that Micala's father might hear of this, but my son made no attempt to temper his enthusiasm. The talk of Jesus captured his imagination in a way I never saw before. When I questioned him, he told me, "I know that the scholars say that Jesus is the fulfillment of all that is written in Scripture. They quote Isaiah and the prophets. I don't know about all that, but there is something in this man Jesus that speaks to every man and woman in Israel. Not just the scribes and scholars, but people like you and me who work hard every day and go to bed exhausted. People who need something to hope for. People who need to feel the presence of God, not just hear about him in conversations. Isn't this what the Messiah is meant to do? To speak to all of us, to redeem all of us?"

Though he was working day and night, my son always took time to converse with our neighbors about Jesus. He was excited as a child when rumor reached us that Jesus would pass through Nain. The preacher kept to no schedule, and no one knew when or even if he might come, but my son redoubled his efforts, hoping to finish the house and send for Micala before Jesus arrived. He wanted everyone he loved to see the one he believed was the Messiah, and I was caught up in his eagerness, I couldn't bring myself to chastise him for his exhausting work pace.

Four mornings ago I heard from our rabbi's wife at the well that Jesus was traveling through the country. It seemed certain that he would pass through Nain and perhaps even stay in the city for a while. Leaving my water jar at the well, I hurried home to tell my son, knowing that although he would be disappointed that Micala would miss this great event, he would be delighted with the news. I rushed into his workshop, my lips already forming the words. Then I stopped.

He lay there, crumpled on the ground, his knees drawn up to his chest; and for a paralyzing moment, all I could see was his father. I found my husband in the same position one evening almost twenty years ago when I went to fetch him from the garden for dinner. When I could breathe again, I walked slowly over to my son's body and fell by his side. The scent of the cedar boards he was cutting for Micala's house hung heavy in the air. I reached out to his face, cold in the morning chill and brushed his hair, still damp, out of his face. Then I touched his forehead and closed his eyes.

I have felt nothing from that moment to this, as I walk slowly beside my son's body. I felt nothing when I learned that Micala's wish were to come and live with me and to give me what comfort she could would not be granted. I waited in vain past the time for the burial that our law called for so that she could be present. Her father's messenger brought word that though she would mourn my son for a year, they had not yet been formally engaged. In good time, Micala would marry the man of her father's choice. Surely, her father's messenger said, I must understand that the good Pharisee could not sacrifice the opportunity to provide a comfortable future for his daughter. And of course, the dowry would not be paid. I heard the words numbly, thinking that my husband's name would now die out in Israel, and that I would be impoverished because my faithful son had used our savings to build a house that would never be used. I felt nothing when I imagined the girl's tearful face as she gazes at the walls of her father's estate, now truly her prison.

I felt nothing when the city gathered around me this morning to help bear my son's anointed body to the burying ground outside our gates. And I feel nothing now when I see the large crowd approaching us on the road. I know in my mind that this is Jesus, finally coming to us, but my heart feels nothing. I think fleetingly that I should go the great man and tell him how my son admired him, but I do nothing. We are about to pass Jesus and the large group of followers when Jesus asks us to wait. I nod listlessly to those bearing the body, beyond caring. Let Jesus look upon this follower whom he has lost.

The man standing before me is about my son's age. I notice his beauty at least. He looks long into my eyes before approaching my son's bier. To my surprise, Jesus steps over and embraces me. The villagers from Nain gasp in unison as he holds me for several moments. When he releases me, I feel my deep heart ache and the warmth of tears. They soak my parchment cheeks as I watch Jesus turn to the bier. He glances at me once more and smiles.

"Do not weep." Then he touches the cot and says, "Young man, I say to you, rise!"

My son sits up and speaks. "Mother." And Jesus, the Messiah, helps my son from the funeral bier and gives him into my arms.

And now I feel everything.

Active Meditation

What would your life be like if a loved one died? Would you simply mourn or would you also have regrets? The widow of Nain was blessed in that both her son and her husband knew how much she loved them, and she knew how much they loved her. They were open and frank in their mutual expressions of love. Choose someone from among your family or friends and express your love for him or her. Select a person who is least likely to know about your love, perhaps because of a conflict or a long separation. Whatever the reason for the estrangement, put it in the past and tell this person of your love. If you are unable to say it, write a letter or send an email. In any case, avoid being stopped by past recriminations, explanations, or defenses. Simply make sure the person knows of your love. That is your simple, and yet difficult, objective.

Reflection/Discussion Questions

1. If you had been in the mourning procession with the widow of Nain, what would you have said to try to comfort her?

2. When you think about your death or the deaths of those you love, are you comforted by the belief that you will be united in the resurrection? Explain how your faith helps you form your thoughts on this.

3. Jesus raised the widow of Nain's son before he raised Lazarus. Why do you think the latter miracle has been given so much more attention and weight?

CHAPTER IV

The Samaritan Woman

Prophet to the Nations

JOHN 4:4–42

As I trudge with my water jar to the village well, I see a woman returning from the well. She must have been late; all the other women come in the morning to draw water, and it is now nearly noon. I wonder, what has made her late this morning? Probably some unreasonable demand by her jealous pig of a husband, whom she cowers before as if he were Caesar himself. Granted, he is a leader in the village, but I detest seeing any woman bullied. And now the little wretch sees me coming, but lacking the advantage in numbers of her sharp-tongued friends at this late hour, she looks away without daring to meet my eyes. Though she must cross my path, she gives me a wide birth, lest passing too close to me infect her.

I laugh loud enough for her to hear me, but it is a hollow laugh. She and the other women, the wives and fiancées and daughters of my village Sychar, have won their war against me. Any small triumph like this one is meaningless. The women have successfully driven me from their company, knowing full well what sorrow it is for a woman to be banished by her own. My only recourse is to laugh mockingly as if I don't care. I do care, but I also put on an excellent show. I will not give them the satisfaction of knowing how they wound me.

The people of Israel disdain us Samaritans; they even think we are unclean. The Jews refuse to touch anything we use. I would be better treated if I lived among Jews, though. At least by living with the Jews, I would avoid rejection by my own people. As it is now, I travel to this well just outside Sychar that our father Jacob built for us, knowing that I will always be anathema among my people.

It is simply because I am not like them that they despise me. I suspect, though, that it is more fear than hate. What would happen to their precious marriages if I, "the one who steals men," as I've heard them call me, set my glance on any one of their husbands? How long would it take for their worlds to unravel as mine has so many times? How long would their so very respectable husbands be able to resist my unspoken offer? And for that, I am condemned.

I continue along the path to Jacob's well, slowing my pace in the hot sun. I may as well take my leisure; after all, as long as I am here, no one will come near to disturb me. They taught their children to shun me; the girls, lest they take me as a poor model, and the boys, I suppose, lest they be tempted to ruin their youth. (As if I would have a boy.) Despite these warnings, a few of the bolder children secretly study me with the curiosity that is the inevitable result of their parent's forbidding. I am often tempted to engage them in conversation just to give their mothers fits. This tactic would avail me nothing, and the children would be punished, perhaps severely. I am that bad.

Or so they tell themselves. What have I done to deserve their scorn? I know I had a part in it; I am not so blind or arrogant as to think myself an innocent victim. I have married several men. I earned my reputation of "the one who steals men." I do not steal them. Nor do I work particularly hard to discourage them. Why should I? How is a woman without money or property to survive without a man? I had nothing from my father who could afford no dowry at my first betrothal. I took nothing from any of my five husbands, neither the ones who divorced me nor the one who died and left his property to his sons from his first marriage. The sons, of course, would spare no portion for me. They already resented the beautiful, young woman who "stole" their father from them. So what am I to do to survive, if not marry?

And regardless of what is said of me, I have never asked any man for a divorce. Staying married is how I stay alive, so why would I choose to leave? But it seems that once a man has me, he ceases to want me. My unusual beauty draws men, the only useful gift passed down to me from my parents. Later, once they have me, they think that this beauty should translate into a compliant, obedient nature. Why should they think this? Have I ever misled a man into this conviction? Have I ever let a man think that once married, I would be his slave, abasing myself to meet his every need? No. Yet men seem to read this unlikely message in my dark, liquid eyes and lithe figure, and I never seek to dispossess them of this misguided perception.

The truth is that I am not well suited to marriage, and therein lies the greatest irony. The very thing that I depend wholly upon for my sustenance is the thing that I am unprepared to do well. If a man wants me for my face and figure and clever conversation, why can he not be content with having those things? My face and figure and wit do not change after marriage; it is what the man wants that changes. If a man desires me for attributes that have nothing to do with labor, why does he expect me, upon marriage, to become a working slave, valued no more than his donkey? If he loves me because I am beautiful and gracefully at ease, why then does he wish to ruin my beauty and mar my grace by rude toil and ill treatment?

When I pledge my troth to a man, do I agree to become chattel or a raw-boned mule? I do not. When I marry, do I agree to stifle my wit and remain silent in all situations? I do not. It is unjust, then, to expect me to do these things. And because I will not, sooner or later, the man tires of me. Depending upon the man, there will be many attempts, some even violent, to force me to obey him. But I will not be forced. Some give up sooner, and others later. What follows, inevitably, is a period of complaining and recrimination in which the man becomes like a whining child who has been denied something he was never actually promised.

At some point my husband, having convinced himself that he made a bad bargain (frequently with the help of his family, who probably argued against the marriage from the beginning), begins to talk about divorce softly at first and then more loudly. The papers will be written, and I will be "put away." The reason he will use matters little to me, though I have made it easy for men—and women, for that matter—to accuse me of all manner of things. I have never argued against a divorce or sought more than I brought into the marriage, usually nothing.

Have I been distressed, disappointed even, in all these failed marriages? Certainly. I never marry planning to divorce; I have never sought, nor desired, such an outcome. I have never been other than what I am, and it is for this that I am shunned. Yet I know that what I do expect is unrealistic. No man will ever be as strong and wise as the one I seek. No man will ever give me, as I am, a future. No man will ever recognize the injustice of my world, nor will any man ever seek to right those wrongs. What man can offer me anything at all that is true? The only man who could do such a thing is the Messiah. And how likely is it that I will ever meet the Messiah!

The well is finally in sight, and I am dismayed to see a man already sitting there. He is a stranger, and when I recognize him as a Jew, my heart becomes leaden. The last thing I wish to face right now is more disdain. Though we share some aspects of faith, the Jews hate us. They blithely ignore that our mutual father, Jacob, gave this well to his son, Joseph, and that we use this gift to this day. The Jews also claim that our worship of the Father is not as valid as theirs is because they worship in Jerusalem, and we do not. There are many such matters separating us, and the Jews use these disagreements to condemn us. In my current state of mind, it is no welcome sight to see a Jew reclining at our well.

I approach purposefully, determined not to be poorly treated by any man on this day. If all goes as it should, he will not speak to me, for Jews do not deign to converse with us. As long as he does not speak, I need not look into his face and see his disgust. But before I even have a chance to lower my jar, the man says, "Give me a drink."

I nearly drop my vessel into the well. Why is he even speaking to me? Refusing to be mocked, I respond sharply, "How is it that you, a Jew, ask a drink of me, a woman of Samaria?"

He does not, as I expected (and perhaps even wished) bristle with anger at my discourteous question. Instead, he smiles a little, and I notice that he is a handsome and somehow compelling man. His beauty surpasses mine, and there is a freshness to it that I doubt I possessed even as a girl. His smile is slow and knowing, but not cruel or smug. With the smile still on his lips, he answers easily, "If you knew the gift of God, and who it is that is saying to you, 'Give me a drink,' you would have asked him, and he would have given you living water."

Oh, please. Is he joking now? Are these strange words meant to waken my curiosity, win me over? Well, it's time to show him that he's not dealing with some uneducated, blushing virgin here. I reply, "Sir, you have no bucket, and the well is deep. Where do you get that living water? Are you greater than our ancestor Jacob, who gave us the well, and with his sons and his flocks, drank from it?"

My bold question does not distress him; indeed, his lovely smile widens and something unfamiliar stirs in me. He says, "Everyone who drinks of this water will be thirsty again, but those who drink of the water that I will give them will never be thirsty. The water that I will give will become in them a spring of water gushing up to eternal life."

When he finishes, the most astonishing thing happens: I believe him. And I understand that the unfamiliar stirring within me is hope.

"Sir, give me this water, so that I may never be thirsty or have to keep coming here to draw water."

When I make this request, his smile diminishes, but his eyes still sparkle with gentle amusement. "Go call your husband, and come back."

My breath catches in my throat. For the first time in my life, I am confused and embarrassed. What am I to say now? I cannot imagine introducing the man I now live with to this extraordinary Jew. I should turn and flee. I look again into his eyes, and instead of escaping, I tell a little of the truth, "I have no husband."

His eyes soften. The smile returns as he says with an unlikely combination of compassion and firmness, "You are right in saying, 'I have no husband'; for you have had five husbands, and the one you have now is not your husband. What you have said is true!"

I do something I have not done since I was a child caught in some untruth by my mother, I blush. Before the color fades in my face, I realize the full import of what this man has said and who he is. I don't know why such a man is speaking to me, but I won't lose the chance to question him. My embarrassment gone, I say, "Sir, I see that you are a prophet. Our ancestors worshiped on this mountain, but you say that the place where people must worship is in Jerusalem."

He leans forward and regards me seriously for a long moment. I hold my breath, fearing I went too far in challenging him. As if knowing my thoughts, he nods slightly to reassure me and says, "Woman, believe me, the hour is coming when you will worship the Father neither on this mountain nor in Jerusalem. You worship what you do not know, for salvation is from the Jews. But the hour is coming, and is now here, when the true worshipers will worship the Father in spirit and truth, for the Father seeks such as these to worship him. God is spirit, and those who worship him must worship in spirit and truth."

I gasp softly. My heart races in the sudden quiet. Finally, I cannot keep silent. I venture my innermost thoughts and hopes. "I know that the Messiah is coming (who is called Christ). When he comes, he will proclaim all things to us."

I wait for his reply, my eyes averted. Can he hear the blood thundering through my veins? He says nothing until I raise my face and look at him. Gazing steadily into my eyes, he says simply, "I am he, the one who is speaking to you."

The breath I am holding issues forth in a shaking sigh. I can think of nothing to say. I want to look away from his glowing face and eyes but cannot. A moment, an hour, a lifetime passes this way, and abruptly I hear voices. Even now, I cannot drop my eyes until the man himself, the Christ, turns his face toward the group of men coming down the path. They had been conversing loudly, but one by one they now grow silent as they see me with their master. Most look surprised, a few even outraged, but not one of them utters a word. One man in particular looks as if he is bursting to speak, and I know well what he would say.

Lord, he would remonstrate, why do you speak to this half-breed, this Samaritan, this woman whose presence here at this well at this late hour betrays what she is? No Jew, least of all you, Lord, should engage with such a person.

I wait for the Christ to send me away, to show his followers that he will not lower himself to the level of a shunned, Samaritan woman. The dismissal does not come. Instead, the Christ looks at the man sternly, with righteous fury in his eyes, and to my amazement, it is the man who looks away, ashamed.

At this I can no longer contain myself. I quickly grasp and release the hand of the Christ, and then, heedless of my water jar, I run back to the center of Sychar. I arrive, breathing heavily, unaccustomed to such exertion, and then I pause to catch my breath. The people in the streets ignore me at first; this is nothing new. Next they look at me as if I have lost my mind. I can imagine what I look like. I, who never leave my house without my face skillfully painted, my hair perfectly dressed and my clothes artfully arranged, am perspiring and disheveled. My breath is heaving like a camel's, as I look around wildly for someone who might believe me.

But who will? Who in Sychar will listen to me or believe my words? Desperate to tell what I know, I feel something I never felt before, true regret for my reputation. As I stand there, hopelessness overtaking my excitement, the woman I passed an hour ago on the way to the well— the one with the brutal, demanding husband—pauses at a market stall. She gazes at me uncertainly, taking in my sorrow. I look at her with a plea in my eyes, and slowly, as if compelled against her will, she approaches me. Despite or perhaps because of his arrogance, her husband is a respected man in Sychar. When this woman comes toward me, others stop to watch. A few exchange troubled glances, and then follow her. Soon, a small group has gathered around me. The woman looks at me with a gentleness I have never seen in another woman's eyes, and she inclines her head as if to invite my speech.

I take a deep, trembling breath and say in a voice so soft and ragged I barely recognize it as my own, "Come and see a man who told me everything I have ever done! He cannot be the Messiah, can he?"

A coarse merchant, who did not leave his stall when the others gathered around me, calls out loudly, "Who doesn't know everything you have ever done, woman?" He snorts with laughter, and I bow my head knowing I have failed. Yet no one joins his laughter. The woman, who first came to me, answers the lout in a clear voice, "How would a stranger know her? And if he were not extraordinary, why would she subject herself to our ridicule this way? Who can say how the Father will choose to speak to us? I myself will go and see this man, lest I lose an opportunity to know the truth."

Her courage astonishes me. Where she goes the crowd will follow, but I know that her husband will punish her if this visit is for naught. He does not want to have a foolish wife, and she may pay the price of his shame. Though I know in my soul that I am right about the man at the well, I give this woman a look of deep gratitude. I want her to know I understand the risk she is taking.

A great crowd follows us back to where the Christ still sits, talking with his disciples. A few men recoil at the advance of such a large number of abhorred Samaritans, but they have learned their lesson and dare not protest. When we draw very close, I step aside so that my people can meet the Master. I feel suddenly reticent, as if I had done a wondrous thing for which I must not claim credit. As the people of Sychar crowd around him, I retreat further still. But then there is a pause in the low talk of the group, and I look up to see the Master, smiling widely, beckoning me to join him in the midst of the people.

I move forward, and when I am seated at his feet, he begins to teach us.

Active Meditation

Do you listen for the many ways God speaks to you? Are there people who bring the face of Jesus to you in ways you fail to recognize? Not every messenger wears a nametag or bears a clerical title. God's message may sometimes be less evident in your pastor's sermon than in the announcement by a reputedly "wild"

movie star who works to prevent famine in Africa. It may sometimes be easier to see the face of Jesus in the deli clerk who has a
pierced nose and tattoos than in the religious sister who runs the
convalescent home where your mother lives. Make a list of every
messenger who crosses your path. Watch and listen for each of
them. Include the monsignor who presides at your daughter's
confirmation and the bank clerk who is so patient with elderly
customers. List the choir soloist who sings "Amazing Grace," but
do not forget the rock musician who donates concert proceeds to
AIDS prevention. When you are feeling cynical or depressed
about the state of the world, consult your list.

Reflection/Discussion Questions

1. Many of her townspeople thought ill of the Samaritan woman.
    With what you know of her background, would you characterize
    her as a survivor, a prophet, or in some other way? Why would
    you describe her this way?

2. Have you encountered anyone in your life who has surprised you
    by showing you the face of Jesus? How did that person affect
    you?

3. Why do you think Jesus chose a Samaritan woman as a messenger?

CHAPTER V

Daughter

'Your 'Faith Has Healed You

MARK 5:21–43

The woman in my arms writhes in pain, grinding her teeth to keep herself from crying out, and I murmur soothing words as I wipe the sweat from her pale, lined face. She has suffered for years with this unbearable pain. There is little I can do but swab her brow with this cool, damp rag and try to keep her calm. She is one of the sick whom I visit, bringing a poultice here, a lotion there, some wine and water to that one, nothing but my presence to another. I have been doing this for almost a year now, and though it is little enough, I know that I leave these sufferers more at ease than when I come.

I can understand them in a way that even some physicians cannot. Like them, I once felt the ravages of unrelenting pain from a disease that no one could diagnose. I know what it's like to think that the long night will never end. I know what it is like to be devastated when the sun finally rises after a sleepless night of pain. The people I visit know that I understand, and that alone, I think, helps them.

Even if I cannot perform a miracle for them, the way a miracle was performed for me, I can at least soothe them with my presence and

43

tell them about the one who healed me. They all like to hear me tell of the miracle, and no matter how many times I repeat it, they always ask for it again on my next visit. Many of them are even able to sleep a little when I finish. I begin now to say the familiar words to this poor woman.

"I was as near despair as one can be and still be alive. And life itself was hardly worth the effort in my state. For twelve years every one of my days was filled with anguish. There were entire days when cramping pain was all that I knew as my blood drained away, taking my life and strength with it. When I was not in clenched over in agony, I was weary beyond words. As strange as it may seem, the times when the pain left me came to be the most difficult because I knew the pain would return. These brief periods of respite were both times of extreme relief and extreme dread: I had a moment to know what a pain-free life could be like, but I knew that the peace and joy would be short-lived. Somehow this respite was as hard to bear as the pain.

"No one could name my malady. I had been to physician after physician. I had been to healers, rabbis, and midwives. None had helped, though some were very happy to take my money in the pretense of curing me. I only grew worse, year after year, and the times of respite grew less frequent. The ones who claimed to know what ailed me were the cruelest, even when they meant to do me no harm. By offering hope, hope that inevitably proved false, they brought me lower than before. Unspeakable disappointment was added to my pain until I could hardly speak in my sorrow and desperation.

"My husband died shortly before the disease took hold. It was as if my grief turned my body inside out, as if it my whole body wept in pain and grief. As much as I miss him, I am grateful to God that my husband never saw me twisted in torment. Although he was a strong man physically, my husband could barely stand the sight of tears, never mind pain. My two daughters had to do no more than let their young eyes fill with tears and my poor husband would give them whatever they wanted or forgive them whatever transgression he had meant to punish. He was like clay in their hands; his heart was so soft. At least he was spared seeing me suffer.

"My daughters are strong in spirit like me, and they did what they could for me during those twelve long years of misery. Their own husbands must not have been happy about the amount of time they spent caring for me, but if they complained, my daughters never said so. One or the other of the girls was with me each time we went to a new physician. Eventually the money my husband saved so carefully for years was gone, spent on useless 'cures.' I did not improve. My eldest daughter then took me into her home and the youngest paid for every physician who promised help.

"It is almost impossible to describe what it is like to suffer constantly and then to hear someone say that healing is possible. No matter how many times the healers failed in the past, each new promise awakened hope, a hope that was almost as searing as the pain. After each failure I would tell my daughters, 'No more. I must bear this illness as best as I can. No longer will I turn to physicians. The sorrow is too much to bear when they fail.'

"We would agree, each of us exhausted with spent hope. Time would pass, and we would hear of a new physician, a new treatment. At first I would refuse to consider it, but then a particularly difficult week or month would pass, and I would begin to think, 'What if this is the one who can help me?' My daughters would sigh and nod and find the money to take me to the new healer.

"A year ago, I finally gave up. I went to a physician who gave me a purging medicine that nearly killed me. I couldn't keep food down for nearly a month, and my daughters had to feed me nothing but honeyed water, a few drops at a time. It took me three months to return to my former state…of continual pain. When I told my daughters I was finished with seeking a cure, I meant it. I think they were relieved.

"I seldom left my eldest daughter's house after that. I did my best to help her around the house and with my two grandchildren, but there was little I could do that was useful. Both my daughters made an effort to include me in their lives, but I grew lonely and depressed. My only social intercourse outside my family was an occasional visit by other widows from the neighborhood. They brought me news and a diversion from my discomfort.

"Increasingly these widows spoke of a preacher or a prophet (depending on who was speaking) called Jesus of Nazareth. Astonishing things were said of this man. Some even dared to suggest that he was the Messiah. Most of the Pharisees denied this claim, but many people were interested in Jesus. Even my son-in-law, normally a taciturn man, spoke enthusiastically of Jesus: 'He preaches more to those of us who work every day for our bread than to the Pharisees in the temple. And he calls us blessed for our struggles here on earth. It is said that he offends the scribes and Pharisees in Jerusalem every time he opens his mouth, and yet the crowds flock to him.'

"I began to look forward to these reports on Jesus. My daughter's husband was not the only one who spoke well of Jesus. Another young man in our city had traveled far to hear him firsthand. The boy returned thrilled with what he heard. The preacher, he told anyone who would listen, spoke in parables, telling stories that every man and woman could understand, talking of lighting lamps and the sowing of seeds and the growth of the mustard plant. This boy was so impressed by Jesus that he left his family soon after to follow him. His parents, worried about the grandchildren they might never have, tried to dissuade him. The boy would hear and talk of nothing but Jesus.

"How I wished I could meet and follow this man. How foolish of me! An old woman, bent with pain and weariness, following after an itinerant prophet. And yet I dreamt of such a thing. I dreamed, too, of having my strength back, lifting my grandchildren in my arms, keeping house for my daughters, and being useful again. And yes, going to sit on a grassy hillside and hearing this unusual man for myself.

"More stories of Jesus reached us, and these new reports interested me more than anything I had heard before. People said that Jesus could heal and could banish evil spirits from the bodies of those they tortured. Word reached us that in Capernaum's synagogue an unclean spirit had called Jesus the 'Holy One of God' just before Jesus cast the evil spirit out. There was talk of a mass healing at the house of his disciple Simon, a healing that began with Jesus raising Simon's mother-in-law, a woman of my own age and health. In Galilee Jesus made a leper clean. People could talk of little else.

"And then came the amazing tale of how, back in Capernaum, the friends of a paralyzed man were so desperate to bring him before Jesus that they removed the roof on the house where Jesus was teaching. The men carefully lowered the paralytic down on a mat before Jesus. When Jesus saw the strength of the faith of the man and his friends, he publicly forgave the man's sins and then told him, 'I say to you, stand up, take your mat and go to your home.' And the paralyzed man did just that.

"I heard that Jesus spent a good deal of his time in seaside cities, often preaching near the shores where people could gather in great numbers. Although I said nothing to my daughters, I secretly yearned to hear him. Would he ever come close enough for me to see him? It was just a dream. I could barely walk anymore. The flow of my blood could come anytime, making it difficult for me to leave our home for any reason. I would have to be satisfied hearing about Jesus and knowing that he traveled and taught at no great distance from where I lay. And I did take some comfort in that.

"Then we heard a shocking report. Across the sea from us, in Gerasene, Jesus performed a miracle that had both frightened and excited people all around the region. When he came to the shore of Gerasene, a man possessed by many demons came from the tombs and accosted Jesus. The demons in the man begged the preacher to leave them alone. The tormented man was covered with cuts and bruises. Jesus felt sorry for this man and began to cast the demons out. The demons begged Jesus to send them into a herd of swine on the mountain. When he agreed, the demons entered the swine and then the entire herd rushed off the cliff into the sea. The people of Gerasene were so frightened by this that they asked Jesus to leave.

"This was all stunning in and of itself, but the news that came next wholly captured my attention. Jesus returned to our shore by boat and was now traveling in our neighborhood. He was near enough to see. I could barely contain myself. What could I do? Could I ask my daughters to bring me out into the way, to leave me on the path where Jesus was likely to pass by? The idea sounded ridiculous even to my fevered mind. Still, I knew in my heart, in my soul, that this was my only chance. I knew that all the other attempts to heal me had been in vain and that this man could make me well. I had never been so convinced of anything in my life. What was I to do? Our neighbors said that Jesus would soon pass by on the way to heal the very sick child of Jairus, a leader of our synagogue.

"I looked up to see my son-in-law, the one who had grown so enamored of Jesus, watching me closely. I looked away. I was embarrassed that I already asked so much of this quiet, good man, and I worried that he knew my selfish thoughts. He gave me one of his rare, sweet smiles—I know it was that smile that my daughter fell in love with—and he said simply, 'Come, Mother.' He carried me outside. The street where Jesus would pass was nearly a mile away, and he carted me the whole distance. When I protested, he replied, 'You weigh nothing.' And that much was true; my body was wasted.

"I heard the crowd before we saw them. There was a multitude of people in the road, all pressing toward Jesus as he walked slowly along the street. Poor Jairus, fearful for the health of his child, tried to disperse the crowd, but Jesus walked at his own pace, the crowd surrounding and reaching out to him. My hope plummeted. We would never come close enough to the healer to even be noticed in this crowd. But my son-in-law, as if again reading my mind, said, 'Courage, Mother!' and then waded into the crowd, holding me in his arms.

"We were so close to Jesus. As Jesus passed directly in front of us, my sturdy son-in-law was pummeled by the crowd and stumbled. I toppled forward against the crush of bodies, and there, on my knees, thinking, 'If I but touch his clothes, I will be made well.' I stretched out to Jesus' cloak as it trailed behind him and grasped the edge.

"A surge of heat and light! A tingling traveled from my fingertips into my very core. Dry, clean air, like a warm wind, swept through my body. I felt the blood flow dry up and disappear. And the pain stopped. Both, I knew, were gone forever. By the time my son-in-law helped me to my feet, Jesus stopped abruptly. Turning and looking all about him, he asked, 'Who touched my clothes?'

"Jesus' disciples, those gathered most closely around him, looked incredulous at his question and observed, 'You see the crowd pressing in on you; how can you say, 'Who touched me?'

"I trembled both from fear and from the sharp, brilliant power of the healing. Jesus looked around, still determined to see who had taken his power from him without asking permission. I stepped forward, and falling down before him, I told him everything. I told him how I hemorrhaged for twelve years. How I spent all my means on physicians and false cures only to grow more ill. How I heard the wondrous reports about him with growing hope. How I fell behind him and touched his cloak, knowing that such a touch would cure me. How I was cured. When I finished, the entire crowd was hushed, waiting. I could not bring myself to look into his face, or indeed, to raise my eyes from the ground.

"In the silence, I felt strong hands on my arms and was lifted to my feet. I looked into the loveliest face. Still holding my arms, he smiled beautifully and said, 'Daughter, your faith has made you well; go in peace, and be healed of your disease.'"

Though this was the end of my story, Jesus' work that day had just begun. They say that he went on from there and raised Jairus' little daughter who had died while Jesus stopped to heal me. His enemies say that the girl was not truly dead and that Jesus could not have raised her, but I believe he did. I know he did. And when I tell this story of my healing to those very ill people I visit, I am always sure to include this part: how he raised the child. I want them to know that if they are never as blessed as I was to meet Jesus in life, he can still raise them from death. He will.

In the months that have passed since that day, I have devoted my life to the sick in our region, when I am not cleaning and cooking for my daughter and son-in-law or minding my grandchildren. Jesus has gone on to do many new and amazing things, and more and more people are convinced he is the Messiah. I believe everything: that he was seen walking on the sea in a storm, that in Gennesaret the sick from the entire region were laid in the marketplace and healed when they touched his cloak (as I had done), that thousands who went to hear him were fed with a few scraps, that he healed a Gentile woman's sick child without even seeing the girl, that a blind man in Bethsaida and a deaf, mute man in the Decapolis were healed by his spittle.

I learned that Jesus offends our leaders in Jerusalem and the Romans who occupy our land. I also believe this. Every miracle is a source of irritation for them because every miracle swells the number of his followers. Jesus seems bent on challenging the jealous, frightened leaders to reconsider their priorities. Again and again, he has humiliated the scribes and Pharisees, mocking their hypocrisy in keeping the purity laws while ignoring the more important laws. Jesus heals on the Sabbath. He heals Gentiles and preaches to Samaritans. He embraces lepers and whores. He challenges the authorities at every opportunity.

None of this is unintended. Every night as I lay down to sleep, I close my eyes and see the image of him holding me by the arms and smiling into my face. There is wisdom in him. He knows what he is doing, and he knows where it will end. He is the Messiah.

I tell the sufferers I minister to every day about Jesus. It is unlikely that they will meet him, that they will be healed in this life as I have been healed. For that, they grieve. And so I tell them again and again that he has raised the dead. He is master of all things. They need only wait. Because I know how hard it is to wait, I lay my hands gently upon them and soothe them. Can they feel his healing in my hands? I hope so.

Active Meditation

Are you someone who brings Jesus to others? Can people see how much you love God in your eyes and feel it in your touch? It is not easy to be such a person. Life is busy, hard, and complicated. It can be an effort just to get through the day, never mind the extras. If you truly have no time for "extras," make a conscious effort each day to bring Jesus to someone you meet. Compliment a passing neighbor. Tip the waiter at the coffee counter. Buy a sandwich for a panhandler or homeless person. Buy flowers for your spouse. Give credit to a co-worker. Cook a meal your children love. Each day, bring goodness—God-ness—to someone. If you can make another kind of commitment, ask your priest or the volunteer coordinator at a local convalescent home if any elderly or ill person needs a visitor. You might accompany a eucharistic minister or join the home's volunteer program. Whether you spend time reading to the person, praying, or simply talking, focus on bringing Jesus into the room. Visit as often as you can.

Reflection/Discussion Questions

1. How would you compare the state of the hemorrhaging woman to that of someone today who is hoping for a cure for cancer, multiple sclerosis, or another serious illness?

2. What role does your faith play in your own sense of health and well-being?

3. Jesus healed the woman of her flow of blood not long before his own precious blood would flow for the healing of the world. Do you see a connection between these two events. What is it?

CHAPTER VI

The Canaanite Woman

Disciple to the Gentiles

MATTHEW 15:21–28

I remember the moment I heard her first cry. My heart melted in my breast. The labor had been long and difficult, and I was weak and sore and soaked with perspiration. I wanted nothing more than to slip into blessed, relieved sleep. But then I heard her cry, and suddenly my every sense was alive with joy and unutterable love. She was my first child, and though I would have others, the sons my husband's family demanded, I loved her with the love a mother reserves for the first.

My spirit went out to her when I heard that cry, so shrill and lusty for such a tiny, struggling creature. The midwife had all but given up on her (and me) and yet here she was, screeching with all her breath as though determined to prove how wrong it was to doubt her survival. I was ill for months with some wasting disease the physicians could not name just before I conceived; no one thought this girl would live. My mother-in-law, who watched the child grow in me, said again and again, "The child will be puny if it lives at all." My sister worried, "You have no flesh on your own bones, how will you nourish a child?" The physicians, whom my husband's parents consulted against my will during the illness, warned me not to risk conceiving until I was well for several months.

But I would not wait. My husband was an only son, and his parents were impatient for grandchildren—sons, of course. I was determined to have a child as soon as I could regardless of how weak the illness left me. My husband, eager to please his parents, did not try to dissuade me. His parents, and not necessarily my health, were his primary concern. I never let myself believe that he loved me, not even during our betrothal; love was too much to expect, and I was no fool. I did believe that he was a decent man and one who would treat his children and me well, but I also knew from the beginning that my main value to him was child-bearer.

I decided as soon as my parents told me of the match, that I would be that child-bearer, but I would do it for my own comfort and advantage. If I had no love from my husband, I would have love from my children. There would be many, I assured myself. The children, at least for a time, would be mine. Mine to love, mine to raise, mine to teach, and mine to bargain with, for with each child, especially with each son, my power and status would increase in the family. My children would pull me from under my mother-in-law's domination.

I reminded myself of this during the long, painful labor. The midwife, though hired by my husband's parents, did her best to comfort me. "It will be easier each time," she mumbled, squeezing a wet rag over my face. I feverishly hoped she was right as I licked the cool drops from my lips. If not, I may not live long enough to best my mother-in-law.

My entire pregnancy was spent in the hope that my first child would be a boy. Such a gift to the family would increase my power five-fold. When the midwife told me it was a girl, I sighed, too spent for real disappointment. I began to slip off into a dragging sleep. When I heard her brave, sturdy cry, everything changed. She was so determined to be heard, to declare herself. I loved her spirit. I loved her heart. I loved her courage. I loved her life!

I demanded to hold her, and the midwife scolded, "Now, you are to sleep! All this fuss over a mewling infant. She nearly killed you!" Unspoken were the words, "And, after all this, she's only a girl." I insisted on holding my baby, and finally the woman laid the red, wrinkled, little thing in my arms. She had been screeching the whole time, but now she closed the angry little circle of her mouth and settled herself into the hollow of my shoulder, her small fist closed around my finger. She smacked her lips twice and went off to sleep. And at that moment, I knew that I would do anything, anything, to keep her safe. I would give my life for her.

I nearly did. I named her Danae and set about making up for the lack of interest from her father and grandparents with the intensity of my love. It is not that my husband was wholly indifferent to her; her personality was too strong and too charming to ignore. I would sometimes catch him watching her while she toddled around our house, getting into whatever mischief she could. He would laugh quietly at her antics as she waved her arms in the air and crowed at some imaginary creature, or jabbered in her own inscrutable language, using all the tones and murmurs of an adult.

Once, when he thought I was visiting with his sister, I came home early to see him holding Danae on his lap and talking nonsense right back to her, as I myself sometimes did. I hid myself and watched them. Danae had an uncanny way of making me think she understood this language, both her own indecipherable sounds and mine when I pretended to talk with her. I could see this happening with my husband, and he continued their conversation with a kind of uncertain wonder on his face that was not wholly without concern. A few months later, I bore him his first son, and he paid no more attention to Danae other than to occasionally chastise me, "You should teach her proper words. People will think that she and you are both fools."

His mother never let the matter rest. Pleased as she was with her first grandson, there was to be no reprieve for me as the bearer of such a precious gift. In that foolish hope, I was wrong. "What is wrong with the girl?" she would whine incessantly. "Why doesn't she learn to speak as any other child? I dare not take her off the estate for fear of her babbling. What might people say of us? There is no pleasure to be taken in such a granddaughter."

As if she were capable of taking pleasure in anything, the old harridan. No, her lack of pleasure in Danae, whom she never, ever called by name, had nothing to do with her complaints. She blithely ignored her daughter's girls as well, taking no apparent pleasure in them either. The difference with Danae is that she took an active interest in my daughter, tormenting me with criticisms and insinuating remarks. By the time Danae was seven, I had borne two other sons, but my mother-in-law's greedy attention would not be sated with three grandsons. Danae still had not begun to speak clearly, and her grandmother was merciless about it.

I tried to hide my daughter from her grandparents. I even protected her from her own father when his mother's influence drove him to harangue me about Danae in my daughter's presence. "Watch what you say!" I would snap back at him when he spoke ill of the girl in front of her. "She can hear you!"

"Can she?" he would bellow back. "I see no sign that she sees or hears! Certainly she does not speak understandably. I should not have let you spoil her so. Look what it has led to. She's a fool, a wretch, unable to learn even the simplest word or chore. What good will she be? Who will marry her?"

"She is a child!" I would whisper back in outrage. "Her marriage is not in question here!"

"Nor will it ever be in the state she's in!" He would leave the house and go to his mother, probably to satisfy his mother with some untruth about Danae's improvement. Even in my anger, I did not envy him that task. I knew that my mother-in-law, despite my bearing three sons, would have easily sent Danae and me away. It was only my husband who prevented it. His ranting at me was more his own fear about our daughter than his rage at me. If only he knew the truth, his fear would turn to terror.

Danae was becoming harder and harder to control. Though she still loved me as much as she was capable of loving anyone, I could see daily in her the struggle between loving me and retreating into the shadows of her life where she seemed to be driven. She would look at me, a plea in her lovely amber eyes as if I could bring her back to this world. But when I tried, not knowing myself how to succeed, she would more often than not lash out at me in rage and frustration, sometimes pummeling me with her little fists. With each passing month, she found it harder and harder to stay in the real world, no matter how she was drawn to me and how much she suffered from her compulsion to pull away.

I was too afraid to seek help. I couldn't bring myself to imagine what my mother-in-law would do if she learned the true extent of Danae's malady. I heard that there were physicians right here in Tyre who might help her, but I dared not seek them out nor bring her to them. Besides fearing my husband's parents, I knew there were many charlatans who "healed" in cases like Danae's by beating and starving patients in an attempt to purge them. I would not risk my child.

I seldom took her from our immediate house and garden for fear of what she might do and what people might say. She was now given to violent fits, kicking and screaming out against whatever imprisoned her and then begging me in her wordless language to help her.

These scenes broke my heart again and again. After her fits I would secretly weep for hours while holding her thin, limp body in my arms. She would always fall into an insensible sleep. I couldn't bear the thought of one of her fits happening in front of others, especially in front of one of the many women who would be only too pleased to carry the tale back to my husband's mother.

I managed to keep the worst of it from my husband because he was seldom in our home except for the early morning and late evening, the times when Danae was usually at her calmest. Though I could not prevent him from hearing her nonsensical language, I managed to feed her separately so that he was exposed to his daughter as little as possible. At first I half hoped he would protest, resisting this separation from the child who gave him such pleasure in her infancy. But he did not. After the birth of his sons he seemed almost relieved to be free from any contact with Danae.

Two years after the birth of our third son, my husband suggested that he and the boys go to live in the large compound of his parents. I swallowed the wild cry of protest that burst from my heart to fill my throat and mouth. He watched me for a long while as I struggled with my anguish. When I finally raised my eyes to meet his, I understood that a bargain had been struck. If I wanted to protect my daughter, I must relinquish my sons. I stared at him for many moments, hoping to see mercy or at least the knowledge of the horrible idea he proposed, but there was no softening in his eyes.

The next day my husband and sons went off to live with their grandparents, the two older boys chattering in excitement of all the pleasures their grandmother had already promised them. My husband carried my youngest boy, only recently weaned. He looked back at me briefly, muttering that he would see me upon occasion, but his voice wavered. He looked away quickly and followed the boys without another word, and I understood that was the extent of the tenderness he had left for me. As I went back in to Danae, I knew it would have to be enough.

Eventually, despite my wrenching sacrifices and best efforts—and I was an expert at concealing and deceiving others in my daughter's interest—I could keep our secret no longer. With no one to help me at the house, I could not avoid taking Danae with me on my furtive visits to the village well and to the market. I tried to go during the times when we were least likely to encounter people and when she was most likely to be peaceful, but it was just a matter of time. Early one afternoon at the well, after I finished filling our jars, Danae was suddenly called into her own world and began to flail around and shout at something only she could see. When I tried to calm her, she struck out at me and knocked one of the jars to the ground, smashing it and spilling the water. There were only three other women at the well, but I vaguely recognized one of them as someone who had been in my mother-in-law's house on some feast day.

Early the next morning as Danae was still sleeping off the exhaustion from the fit, my mother-in-law appeared at my door accompanied by two male slaves from her estate. She strode in without waiting to be invited and demanded flatly, "Let me see the child."

"She is not here," I said swiftly, defensively.

Her lips twisted into what passed for a smile on her sour face. "And where is she then? With her father? But no, for he is in my house with his sons, isn't he? Let me see her!"

Her cruelty took my breath away. When I recovered enough, I said defiantly, "She is sleeping, and I will not wake her!"

"Not even to see her own grandmother?" she asked with the same sickening smile. Turning to the slaves, she said, "Bring her."

I stood helpless as they swept through our small house. She was in my room so that I could watch her through the night. Although I did not follow them, I knew as soon as they found her. Her screams rent the air like a scythe, growing in ferocity when the slaves dragged her into the room. Holding her kicking figure between them, for it took all the strength of two such men, they brought her before her grandmother. Danae contorted her body, twisting to see me and pathetically crying the word that I knew as "Mother." At that, I could bear no more, and moving swiftly, I tore her from their grasp. She came willingly into my arms, but it was a long time before her screams turned to frightened whimpers.

One of the slaves asked his mistress if he should drag the girl back to stand before her, but my mother-in-law, never taking her eyes off my daughter, said only, "I have seen what I came to see." She did not deign to even gaze in my direction as she swept out.

Danae was in turmoil for much of the day and would not eat even a morsel until she finally collapsed just after twilight. I could do little more than curl my aching body around her warm little form. I spent the night feeling her rapid heartbeat and listening to her breathing, which finally became even and clear.

Her father came in before dawn. I was awake (I never truly slept that night) and came softly out of the room to meet him. He did not embrace or greet me, but began speaking immediately, "My mother will come for Danae later, as soon as she arranges for the child to be sent to Sidon. There is a so-called healer there, though his claim is not to heal, but to drive out demons. The last child who was given to him, a strong boy of fourteen, was beaten to death. The parents were convinced that this was the only way to completely 'heal' him."

He stopped and looked at me, as if telling me this horrifying news was all that he had come to do, all that he could do. A scream to rival any that I heard from Danae's mouth, a scream that had been waiting for years formed in my bowels and broke through my lips. I threw myself at him with such fury that he was at first too stunned to defend himself. But as my scream filled the room, he held me with one arm and forced his hand over my mouth with the other. I continued to fight, trying to bite him, but he was strong. I might still have struggled against him, but I looked up and saw the tears streaming down his face. All the life drained from me, and I knew how my daughter must feel at those moments when all her vital energy, was spent. I collapsed into his arms.

Together we wept. I finally said, "You can stop your mother."

"I cannot," he said hoarsely.

"You can!" I cried, pulling away from him and pacing through the room like a caged animal.

"How can I?" he asked in the same wretched voice. "No one can prevent her from doing as she wishes. Could you keep her out of this house yesterday? Could you keep her from Danae? No. She is determined that no stain should touch the name of the family or be associated with our three sons. Nothing will stop her. She says Danae is mad, possessed."

"And you let her speak that way? You are as cruel as she!" I flung the words at him as if they were my fists, but still he kept his temper.

"There is only one thing," he said, and I turned to look at him. "People are talking of a rabbi from Israel, a Jew called Jesus whom they say can heal. He has many healings to his credit. They say he has cured men and women. And children. And they say he drives out demons. That they leave at just a few words from him."

I stared at him, a pulse of hope beating in my throat. "You must go to this man! You must ask him to come to Danae and cure her!"

He said nothing, shaking his head, no. "Why not?" I hissed at him, trying to keep my voice low lest I wake Danae. "You must!"

And now my husband, for the first time, lost his temper. "I will not beg before a Jew!" he shouted, suddenly heedless of our daughter asleep in the next room. "I will not humiliate myself in front of the crowd that follows him everywhere. Never!"

"Then why have you come here?" I asked in a low, spent voice, my newly kindled hope now in ashes.

"You should go to this Jesus. He is said to be traveling even now on the main road through our district. Perhaps he will be gentle with a woman," he said without looking at me. When I said nothing he added, "I will stay with the child."

The child. Not "my daughter." Not "Danae." Just "the child." And I knew then that my husband had done all he could. Without another word, I put on a robe and ran from the house.

And whenever I think of what happened next, it is as if I am living it all over again.

As I run, the sun comes up hot and bright, a bright yellow orb in the sky. I see a crowd on the distant road. I race on ignoring the cuts on my feet and the streaks of dusty sweat on my face. The sun is in my eyes, and I cannot see him clearly, but there is a tall man in a white traveling robe walking in the midst of the group. Before I even reach him, I begin to call out, "Have mercy on me, Lord, Son of David; my daughter is tormented by a demon."

The man walks on, as if I had not spoken at all, and the crowd begins to murmur against me. They are all Jews. I remember my husband's words about not begging before a Jew, but I keep up my shouting, appealing to him in a parched voice he cannot help but hear. I am relentless, and after several minutes, I hear one the disciples closest to him say, "Send her away, for she keeps shouting after us."

Jesus stops and takes a deep breath as though he was disturbed and seeking patience. When he speaks, I am not sure if he is speaking to the crowd or to me. "I was sent only to the lost sheep of the House of Israel."

Whether he is speaking to me or not, I hear something good in his voice, despite the words. I seize the opportunity and fall on my knees before him. "Lord, help me."

Although he answers me, I still feel that he is addressing the whole group. "It is not fair to take the children's food and throw it to the dogs."

The words come to my lips unbidden, "Yes, Lord, yet even the dogs eat the crumbs that fall from their owners' table."

He looks down at me directly for the first time. And for the first time, I can clearly observe him, his light-filled eyes, his kind, gaunt face and tall figure. We gaze at each other for some moments, and it is as if the crowd itself has ceased to breathe. Finally I see a small smile form on his lips and tears in his eyes. In a strong voice meant to carry into the crowd, he says, "Woman, great is your faith! Let it be done for you as you wish." He puts his warm hand on my head for one fleeting moment, and then he is gone, the crowd following.

I stay on my knees for a long time, listening to the sounds of them moving away. When I rise, I feel ancient, sore, and tired. But my heart, for the first time in years, is quiet. I am not sure what I will find when I return, but I know that our suffering is ended. I walk back along the path, my body spent but my spirit at peace.

It takes me much longer to return, and when I enter the courtyard of my home, my heart begins to race. My husband is standing in front of the door facing his mother who is accompanied by yesterday's slaves plus two others. "My son," she commands in a voice more wheedling than the one she used on me, "Give me the child. I will see that no harm comes to her."

My husband says only no, squares his shoulders. He looks, not at his mother, but at the slaves. All four slaves look discomfited, as if wondering what they must do if their mistress orders violence against the young master. I wonder the same thing as the silence lengthens. The air becomes hot, heavy with fury and fear, and none of us notice at first when the door to the house opens. Danae comes and stands beside her father, slipping her small, supple hand into his. I can see him grasp reflexively the little fingers he's never seen unless they were balled into a tense fist. Danae looks up at him and smiles beatifically. She turns her face toward the shocked old woman standing before her and says in a bright, sweet voice, "Good morning, Grandmother. Have you come to visit?"

My mother-in-law, her face crumpling in confused surrender, leans on one of the slaves as they bear her away. My husband does not notice. He is crouched on the ground, holding his daughter's face in his hands, regarding her with joyful astonishment as her fingers hurry to wipe away his tears. Slowly, as if in a dream, I walk toward my family.

Active Meditation

Like the Canaanite woman, many parents face a complicated array of problems and issues. Do you know a parent who is overwhelmed and stressed? Offer that parent a little respite. Volunteer to babysit while the parent (or parents) spend some time away from home, perhaps for a movie, meal, or a mini-retreat. If you can't babysit, offer to pay for a reliable sitter. You might also cook a meal, do grocery shopping, chauffeuring, or laundry, anything that might give the person time to himself or herself.

If you yourself are an overwhelmed parent, make a plan to get some time to yourself. Consider resources you haven't thought about. Can a spouse, friend, or family member help? Can you hire a babysitter? If none of these are options, try to make a "trade" with another parent by offering to care for each other's children, something that can become a continuing arrangement. Plan to do something you really enjoy during this respite. Begin by offering a prayer of thanksgiving to God and end the time by asking God for patience and strength as you resume your responsibilities.

Reflection/Discussion Questions

1. The Canaanite woman risked extreme humiliation, to help her child. Do you think most parents today are aggressive and self-less enough when it comes to protecting and helping their children? Explain your answer.

2. Do you think that Jesus was truly astonished at the woman's faith, or was he deliberately using her as an example of how "Gentiles" should be welcomed in the church? How do you or groups you belong to welcome strangers, those who are "different"?

3. Were you surprised by Jesus' initial remarks to the woman? How would you explain them?

CHAPTER VII

The Mother of
James and John

Pragmatic Prophet

MATTHEW 20:20–28

I always wanted daughters. I might be the only woman in Israel who would admit to such a thing, but it's true. Even before I had my two sons, I wanted a daughter. Oh, don't misunderstand me. I was proud and happy to bear James and John. In this I am no different from every other Jewish woman. I know how important it is to have sons. Sons were especially important for my husband, a fisherman, who needed them to help him with his business. I know he hoped that they would take over the business one day.

I was pleased when my sons came one after another in the first few years after we married. My husband, Zebedee, was pleased with me and showed this in his own rough way by hiring a girl from the village to help me after each pregnancy. When his business was established, we had a daily servant to help me run the household and garden. But secretly, I still yearned for girls. I had grown up among brothers, and my mother had been overwhelmed with the constant process of feeding and caring for them to spend much time with me. As a result, I was a solitary child. I learned early how to speak up for myself; it was the only way I could get even a small amount of attention in our boisterous house.

I often did the things my brothers did. I always tried my best to stand up to my brothers and competed with them for my mother's attention. Still, at the end of the day my mother had little time for me. She was able to teach me only the rudimentary things expected of a Jewish girl. I even resented my brothers' opportunity to study the Torah and begged my father to let me join them. He would just laugh good-naturedly and send me away, as if such a request was too ludicrous for a response. I might have turned to the other girls in our village for companionship, but I was considered so loud and strong that they avoided me. I didn't know how to act like a girl; I longed for sisters or someone to teach me.

Fortunately my parents found a husband for me who was not put off by my forward ways. Indeed my husband appreciated my strength and sturdy spirit and often said that I was the perfect fisherman's wife, especially when I bore him two healthy sons. And after I did my duty by my husband and family, I eagerly anticipated my next pregnancy, certain I would finally have a girl. I told myself that I would not be like my mother, that I would nurture and appreciate my daughter and teach her everything I learned as a woman.

As time passed and I didn't become pregnant again, my hopes took on a deeper urgency. Could it be that after all this time, all this dreaming, I was to be denied the daughters for whom I waited my whole life? I talked to one of my sisters-in-law about my fears, but she with three daughters and no sons had little understanding or sympathy for me.

"Salome, how can you complain of having no daughters, when you have two strong, healthy sons?" she chastised me irritably, watching John and James playing at the water's edge while they waited for their father to return from fishing. Dismissing my problems, she went on, "You cannot imagine what it is like to be a wife who cannot bear sons, especially a wife married to your brother. It is all he talks about. 'My mother had nothing but sons, and you cannot bear even one,' he rants at me. 'It is not from me that this malaise comes. I have sons in my blood, but all you give me is daughters. And how am I to pay to marry off these daughters without sons to work and support us?' He goes on and on and gives me no rest. And you think you have something to feel sorry about? Compared to most women, you are blessed!"

Despite her harsh lack of sympathy, my sister-in-law brought me to my senses. She was right: I was blessed. I looked at my sons, so strong and happy, and in the distance I could see my husband's boat against the horizon. He had tried so many times to comfort me when I grew morose about our lack of daughters. As often as not, I would push him away in my sorrow and frustration. Small and unknowing as they were, even my sons shied away from my moods and became confused by my inexplicable coldness. What had I been doing? God had given us everything, and here I was, mourning something I had never really known.

From that day, I relinquished my dream of daughters and concentrated on my sons and husband. As they grew, my sons gradually became aware that their mother could do things that other mothers couldn't do, such as lifting them into the air and swinging them about or wading into the sea to help pull in a net heavy with fish. While other mothers were sewing and kneading bread, I was mending nets and teaching my boys to swim so they would be better able to work safely with their father. My sons' pride in their mother made up for whatever small loss I still felt.

As my sons became men, I began to think I would have daughters-in-law (almost as good as daughters). Besides, they might give me granddaughters. Both John and James were considered "good catches" themselves. The mothers in Capernaum looked on my sons with happy speculation, yet neither John nor James seemed to be in a hurry to marry. My husband approved of this caution, wanting both boys to be well established before starting a family, but I was growing anxious. Had we made our sons so comfortable at the hearth of our home that they would lag behind in starting their own families? When I brought this thought to Zebedee, he just looked at me and said in exasperation, "Salome, is there anything you can't worry about?"

Abruptly one day all this conjecture became meaningless. My sons and their father had been fishing with my husband's partner and his two sons, Simon and Andrew. The boys had long been friends. They grew up together and had all the changing alliances that boys have, complete with fisticuffs and forgiveness. Though my husband and their father had worked together for years, they would officially join the two businesses when all four sons married and began their own families. Simon had already married a wife and moved into his own house. The six men went out into the sea at least twice every week, often relying on each other for protection from the quick storms that blew so violently across the Sea of Galilee. And when one boat had a catch too great to bring in, the other always helped. Likewise, if one partner and his sons had a fruitless trip, the others would share their catch.

This morning neither partner had caught anything at all, which was unusual. I could see from our garden, which looked out to the sea, that all six men were downcast. My husband's shoulders sloped with fatigue and disappointment. Though he would not admit it, he was worried. The catches had been poor lately. We had a good deal saved, but he worried that the small fleet could not support six families, not to mention the hired men who depended upon the business for income and food. My husband conferred with his most experienced hired man while John and Andrew stayed in the boat mending torn nets. When I looked toward the other boat, I saw Simon and Andrew in conversation with a stranger. He was a tall, white-robed man, thin from what I could see. Simon became very animated as they talked. Of course Simon was always animated, so that was no real cause for concern.

Next I saw a large group of people lingering close by, as if follow-ing the stranger. They seemed unsure whether or not they should interrupt him as he conversed with Simon. I had heard that a so-called prophet was preaching in the region and wondered if this man was the one everyone was speaking about. Preachers seemed to be everywhere in Galilee these days, always promising deliverance from the Romans who had oppressed and taxed us for so long. None of them had brought such deliverance. They were all talkers, shouting useless words at men like my husband and sons who worked for a living as men should. This preacher was probably no different than the others, and I felt sorry for the fools standing about idle, waiting to hear him. They would do better working than fol-lowing a preacher who could do nothing for them, much less put food in their mouths.

Eventually Simon gestured to his boat, and when the man got in, Simon pulled away a little from the shore. The lingering crowd, larger than I first thought, pushed forward to hear the man speak. I contin-ued in my garden, weeding, pruning, and finally gathering what I would need for the evening meal. As I prepared to go in and make breakfast for my sons and husband, I saw the man finish his words and dismiss the people. They left reluctantly, and then Simon spoke again with the stranger.

Suddenly Simon turned around and prepared the boat as if he would go out again. His father shook his head in disgust and left the shore, trudging in the direction of his house. As Andrew joined Simon in the boat, I hurried along the path to my sons and husband. "What is this?" I asked quietly so as not to offend the stranger, who stood intently watching Simon and Andrew put the boat back out. John said nothing, but his eyes were fixed on the stranger. James said with a small, mocking smile, "This man called Jesus told Simon that if he went back out, he would make a great catch. Simon told him that we had been fishing all night with nothing to show for it, but the preacher insisted. And you know Simon, he'll do anything if there's a chance of a good catch. Their father wants nothing to do with this."

"And who could blame him?" said my husband, his own face dark with annoyance. "We have not even seen a fish all night, and now at the word of this stranger, we should put back out? We have no time for such foolishness."

"But Father," said John tentatively, "You heard this man speak just now. His words…"

He was interrupted by a great shout from Simon, well off shore by now. Simon was gesticulating like a madman, beckoning to my sons and husband for help. Even from this distance, we could see that the nets were ready to burst with fish; their hired man on the shore was no help. The boat was all but sinking, and Simon was shouting in desperation. In the swift way of fishermen who must act or lose, Zebedee, John, and James launched the boat within moments. They reached Simon and Andrew and were able to salvage the great catch. As they slowly made their heavily-weighted way to shore, dragging nets alive with fish, I turned to look fully at the stranger Jesus.

Silent and unmoving, he had watched the boats the whole time. Now he turned to me. His face had a beauty that was unlike anything I had ever seen, and his eyes seemed filled with the sun. When he slowly smiled at me, there was something wistful in his smile that left me feeling as if a chasm just opened inside me. As the men came in and Jesus returned his gaze to them, I also turned back to the boats and saw my son John staring back at Jesus with an expression of such longing and joy it took my breath away. And I realized what it was that had passed between Jesus and myself. His gaze had been an unspoken apology, and the chasm that had opened in me had been the realization that I had lost my sons.

Jesus told my sons and Simon and Andrew, "Do not be afraid; from now on, you will catch people." By nightfall, all four were gone.

My husband was inconsolable. "How could this be?" he kept muttering over and over again, as if there were an explanation that we could ever understand. "They are gone. Gone! What will become of them with this man? What will become of us? Our work? And Simon and Andrew have deserted their father as well."

"All four are men," I answered quietly, as best I could. "They went with him willingly."

"He took them!" Zebedee roared in a rare show of anger. "He showed them some trick, and then he took them!"

"But what trick could this be?" I continued, never one to be afraid of anyone, least of all my husband. "If not from God, how could this miracle happen? You said yourself, there were no fish."

My husband was quiet, and his fury passed as quickly as a squall on the sea. I knew it was not so much anger but confusion that held him, and I tried to comfort him. "We have a great deal saved against a crisis, though we could not have imagined such a thing as this. Still, we are well-off, and you could leave fishing altogether if you wish."

"I do not wish!" he cried, though more in fear than anger. "And that money we have saved was for John and James to establish themselves, take wives, and have children. Are we to spend it while they journey back and forth across the country with this man? Are we never to have daughters-in-law and grandchildren to ease our aging and warm our hearts?"

He struck at my own heart with this last statement; I had looked forward to weddings and grandchildren for a long time. I had to swallow my own grief to answer him. "If this Jesus is not true, the boys will return. John is easily smitten, I know, but James has good sense and will soon see through any trickery. If this is really trickery."

"You doubt that it is?" Zebedee asked morosely. "You believe what they say about this preacher being the Messiah, then?"

"Husband, I do not know. But I mean to find out."

"And just how will you do that, wife? Leave our home and follow the man yourself?" my husband mocked wearily. When I made no answer, he sat up and looked at me incredulously. "No! Salome! Have you lost all sense? You cannot join that mad crowd, following this man about like a cur seeking a scrap! I forbid it!"

"You forbid it?" I repeated in a low voice that he had come to recognize as a threat to the peace of our home. My husband had never forbid me anything; I was his wife and partner, and I worked harder to support his business and raise his sons than a houseful of servants. Jewish law may have permitted him to forbid me, but the laws of our marriage did not.

After staring at me for a long moment, he looked away and said softly, "Then you, too, will leave me?"

I sat beside him and took his face in my hands. "I will never leave you. But we must know what has happened to our sons. I must know. Come with me! The fish have not been running, and we can go together, at least for a time."

But he was already shaking his head no. "My whole life is here, in this village, by this sea," he said sadly. I knew he was right. I held him in my arms through that night; by morning, we decided that I would join those who followed Jesus as long as he stayed in this region and I could return home at night to be with my husband.

And so it went for some months. I never traveled far from home, but what I saw astonished me. Jesus cleansed lepers and made a paralyzed man walk. He made another man's ruined hand whole again so the man could go back to his work and support his family. I saw him drive out unclean spirits and even heal slaves and Gentiles. But these healings were not all I saw and heard. Jesus taught a whole new way of living, a way that stunned the leaders of our nation and faith. He taught that we were to love not just our friends and families, but our enemies as well. He claimed that he was "lord of the Sabbath." He called the poor and the hungry and the grieving "blessed." He healed on the Sabbath, heedless of how he enraged the Pharisees.

Soon I was as attracted to Jesus as were my sons. How could I be anything else, seeing what he did, listening to his words? I also realized that my sons were not coming home. As long as Jesus could be followed, they would follow him. And they would go wherever he led, of that I was sure. I told Zebedee as much, and though he resisted this truth at first, eventually he became resigned. But he never joined us when we traveled with Jesus; that he could not bring himself to do. And he resisted when I first came to him with the request for money to support Jesus' work.

"Is it not enough that I lose my sons—and it seems, my wife—to the man? Now I must give him my savings as well?" he asked angrily. "Should I remind you that these savings were meant for my sons and grandchildren?"

Ignoring his remark about losing his wife, for he knew that it was not true, I said softly, "There will be no grandchildren, my husband. They follow Jesus, and that is all they care about now. There is nothing else on their minds. Is it not better for us to give them their money now, to support this man who has become their life? He is the Messiah."

"And what does it take to be the Messiah?" asked Zebedee. "Will he drive out the Romans with his talk of love and forgiveness? Will he show us the face of God?"

"He is the face of God. Your sons believe this, and so do I. And yes, of course, he must drive out the Romans; how else will he become king of Israel?"

"Yet you've told me he talks of his own death." My husband was not easily convinced. "What king welcomes his own death?"

"It is not that he welcomes it," I responded, not sure myself what Jesus meant by such talk. "I have not heard him myself on this; I only repeat what I heard from Peter and John and James. But I believe he means to say that he would die, if need be, for Israel and the Father, not that he must die. And what king would say anything different?"

In the end Zebedee gave me a purse and from that I helped support my sons and the work of Jesus. I was frequently with those who followed him; his mother, Mary, was often kind to me. We were a group of women who did what we could to advance his work, and we grew close. I stayed with my sons when we traveled. Although I mourned that I would not have grandchildren, I took consolation in being so much a part of my sons' lives. I felt blessed to regain the closeness we lost when the boys grew up and took to the sea.

One night, over our evening meal, my sons continued an argument they must have started earlier in the day. "He will do this for us, if only we ask," John, his voice tense with excitement, told James. But James merely shook his head wearily, reminding me so much of Zebedee in that moment that I was struck with a pang of yearning for my good, solid husband. James said, "John, listen to yourself! We cannot ask such a thing of him. Can you not see that such things as place and power mean nothing to him?"

I interrupted them, "What are you speaking about?"

John, as usual, was unable to restrain himself and jumping up, started pacing without answering me. James regarded him silently for a moment before answering, "John wants to ask Jesus to reserve two places for us, so that we might sit beside him when he becomes king of Israel."

I was not surprised. John had always been impulsive, given to passion and quick judgment. I knew that he worshiped Jesus and that nothing would make him happier than for everyone to know he was Jesus' leading disciple. James was more reserved, more given to quiet thought, and so I asked him, "And you do not agree with your brother on this?"

"Of course not!" John burst out. "He thinks we will seem grasping and ambitious, that Jesus will think poorly of us. But how does it reflect poorly on us if all we want is to be beside him always?"

James muttered, "That's not how he'll see it, nor how the others will see it."

"Who cares what they think?" John demanded irritably.

I understood James' concern. Unlike John, he had always been aware of how Jesus appeared both to his followers and to his enemies. It seemed now that James was also deeply aware of how Jesus' disciples themselves appeared. He did not want to seem greedy or selfish. Still, after my sons had gone off to sleep, I began to think about what John wanted of Jesus. And why should my sons not have this honor? Had they not given up as much—no, more—than others had? At least Simon, whom Jesus had renamed Peter and who many perceived as the leading disciple, had a wife and family. My sons had neither, and they had given up a lucrative fishing business to cast their lot with Jesus. Weren't my sons more deserving than Levi, who was a tax collector, or Simon, who came from Cana, or even Thomas, who still didn't seem sure of Jesus?

James, too, was right. It was not proper for them to ask Jesus themselves to grant such an honor. It would seem wrong to the others, and perhaps even to Jesus himself. But what if I made the request? Surely everyone would understand how a mother would want the best for her sons. And after all, it was Zebedee and I who had lost daughters-in-law, grandchildren, and our business. I resolved to find an opportunity to bring John's request before Jesus.

The opportunity came a few days later. Only the closest disciples were around Jesus. I arose, walked over to where he sat and knelt before him. Raising my face to his, I asked if he would grant me a favor. He looked at me; his face held the same knowing sadness that I saw on the beach that first day we met. For a chilling moment, I felt that he already knew what I wanted and hoped I wouldn't ask. But before I could back away or make some excuse, he asked me softly, "What do you want?"

I swallowed hard, my confidence gone. Then I remembered my sons and how deserving they were, and I asked, "Declare that these two sons of mine will sit, one at your right hand and one at your left, in your kingdom."

His eyes dropped to the ground in what seemed to be sorrow and disappointment. When he answered, it was not to me that he spoke, but to my sons, as if he knew I asked on their behalf. He began to speak in the same quiet voice, "You do not know what you are asking."

Before he spoke another word, I felt my heart become like a cold stone. I remembered my husband's question, "And what does it take to be the Messiah?" What had I done? Oh, my sons! What had I done?

Active Meditation

Do you have a vocation to serve God and your church in some way? Have you avoided the idea because you're too busy, too involved with work, or afraid of what others might say? Remembering that Jesus' disciples and their families gave up everything to follow him, take the first step toward living your vocation. Investigate what you would have to do to pursue it. This does not mean you must pursue it, but at least find out what kind of time commitment, training, and so on it might take. If you are unable to become a priest, can you become a deacon or eucharistic minister? If you cannot enter a religious order, can you volunteer at a school, nursing home, or hospital run by sisters? Can you be a catechist or an usher or greeter, or pass the collection basket? Can you serve on your church's council or work on the Christmas bazaar? Your research may lead you to an unexpected path; it may be easier than you think to serve.

Reflection/Discussion Questions

1. Why do you think that Jesus' disciples followed him? Was their response to him based on his message of love and forgiveness or because they hoped he would drive out the Roman occupiers and establish an earthly kingdom? Explain.

2. If the mother of John and James, and John and James themselves, had known what they would have to suffer as Jesus' closest disciples, do you think they would have made the same request? Why or why not?

3. If someone close to you told you that he or she had been "called" to leave everything—including you—to follow a poor, charismatic, traveling preacher, how would you respond?

CHAPTER VIII

Joanna

Courage Embodied

LUKE 8:1–3

Even when I wondered how my marriage would survive my faith, I could not bring myself to abandon Jesus. And no matter how loudly my husband complains now, it was he who caused us to be in this inexplicable situation.

Ten years ago no one would have thought it possible that I would become a follower of a man like Jesus, least of all myself. I was a Jewish girl looking for a husband, just like every other Jewish girl of seventeen, at least the ones I knew. It is fair to say that my parents were determined to marry me off as soon as possible. Ours was a traditional family, and my parents wanted a man who would be able to care for me and give them grandchildren.

I rejected Chuza when they first brought his offer to me. He was older than I was, which was not enough of a reason to reject him, but the truth is that I didn't like how he looked. He was not handsome; there was something miserly in his looks. His face was a little too pinched, his eyes a bit beady and bird-like, his flesh a little too spare, his hair and beard already thin. Even his gestures were stingy, as though he consciously avoided moving with extravagance. My parents and older, married brothers, however, were not about to take my no for an answer.

"Do you think you are some beauty, an exotic Egyptian princess, maybe, who can command wealthy, handsome young princes with just a word or two?" my mother demanded sarcastically. "Or, tell me, do you see sturdy, young men of Judea waiting in line outside our door to beg for your hand? What position are you in, Joanna, to say no to this one, when there is no other to say yes to?"

Even then, I had some spirit of my own, and for a while I fought back. "Even if there is no line of men, am I to be married off like a cow to the first wretched creature who makes a proposal? This Chuza looks like a strong desert wind could blow him over! What do I want with such a man? What does he offer to recommend himself? He is nothing but a poor steward!"

"A poor steward in Herod's palace!" my mother retorted. "And with his own quarters right in the palace itself! They are probably more lavishly appointed than anything you've dreamed of, daughter! And you will never have to worry about food—or even cooking, for that matter, since you've shown no skill or interest in that—if you share your bed with the steward who feeds the king of Israel!"

"King of Israel!" I scoffed. "As if any true child of Israel considers that fox our king! Why, my own father, your husband, despises him for his posturing. Herod is anathema and no true Jew. Having heard nothing but ill of him in this house, now I learn you want me to wed one of his craven servants? Will you set me up to be the cause of laughter for all our family and neighbors who deplore Herod as much as my father and brothers? How will you explain that, Mother?"

"We need explain nothing to you!" my father thundered, having entered the house unnoticed. "We are your parents, and you will obey us. Or have you forgotten the Law of Moses? This man, Chuza, has a good living and a good position. What concern is it of mine if he takes his living from that lying fox? Is the food not good? Is the couch not soft? Are the clothes not fine? Does the money not spend like any other money? You will marry this man after Passover."

"I will not," I declared, pressing my lips together and standing straight in a show of determination. I never so blatantly disobeyed my father before, and I had to hide my fear of his reaction. With good cause. My father's face grew hard and red, and he stared at me as if he'd never seen me before, as if some dirty animal had somehow crept into his house and snarled at him. My father had never in all my life raised his hand against me, though he'd beat my brothers. I thought he would surely beat me now. He did not strike me; instead he made a cold, quiet statement that froze my blood more than a beating might have heated it. "You will marry Chuza or you will be sent to your brother's home in the far distant hill country, where you will serve his wife. Choose."

My stomach churned. My brother, an overseer of shepherds in a region so rural and poor it was as if civilization had never touched it, was a reticent man who deferred in all things to his wife. She had lived in Jerusalem like us, and she had never stopped resenting my brother for moving her so far from her family and even from meager comforts. Her rage during the one festival a year when they came to stay with us made the very air shiver and cool. I had always stayed as far out of her way as possible. To compound the matter, she had borne him five children in seven years and seemed to take a grim pleasure in letting the children run wild. Whether she was completely overwhelmed by the little desert rats, or, as I suspected, simply wanted to embarrass my brother (and mother and father during these yearly visits) by allowing the children to do as they wished, my brother never attempted to overrule her or control his brood.

I must go into this miserable household if I refused Chuza. My brother's wife always made a point of being particularly rude to me, believing, as she often said, that I was pampered and indulged at home, just outside of Jerusalem.

My father stood staring at me, while my mother looked away. For all her harshness with me on the matter of my marriage, even she was disturbed by the image of me ending up at the mercy of my sister-in-law and the little monsters she called children.

I left the room and, relying on my mother's intervention, managed to hold out for four days. On the fifth day, my father began to have my belongings packed and told me to be prepared to journey to my brother's rough home after the next Sabbath. My mother either could or would do nothing to save me. At dinner that night, a silent affair like every other meal since our violent confrontation, I said with as little grace as I could manage, "I will marry the man." My father said nothing, but my belongings were returned to my room by the time I retired for the night.

I cannot say that I have learned to love Chuza in the past ten years, but I soon stopped despising him. He was, at first anyway, so pleased to have secured himself a bride that he treated me with kindness and what passed for generosity in his narrow mind. Though I had few of the luxuries my parents had so lavishly described, I was well fed and clothed. Herod trusted no one, but he seemed to have a genuine liking for Chuza, when he took any notice of him at all, and we benefited from this. Our food was always fine with the considerable added advantage that I didn't have to prepare it, since Chuza brought the generous portions that were his due directly from the palace kitchens.

Though I greatly resented not having my own home, our quarters were hung with fine tapestries, the vessels were beautifully made, and we had the use of furniture that even my father could not afford. Still, none of it, even the elegant raiment I wore, was really mine, and I chafed under that knowledge. I grew accustomed to Chuza's stinted ways, but he constantly tried to placate me by pointing out that we lived in much more luxury than my brothers and their wives. Remembering the fate that had awaited me at my brother's house, I did take some comfort in Chuza's words.

Gradually things began to change. Herod brought his brother's wife into the palace to be his own wife. Herod treated her daughter, his niece, as his own. Israel saw this as shameful. The woman herself had no shame. She acted as though she was the queen and demanded that the palace be run at her whim. Herod, who soon tired of her constant harangues, gave her the run of his home, if not his kingdom. The woman was like a tyrant. No slave or servant, not even a highly placed servant like my husband, avoided her critical notice.

Chuza, who had grown confident (if not lazy) in his position, was suddenly nervous. He was accustomed to taking his ease during the day. Sometimes he used to spend an hour or two with me in our rooms; now he could not risk being thought lax in his work. As a result, I barely saw him from the moment he rose in the morning till he returned late at night. If Herod was having a feast—and the woman who called herself his wife demanded that he have many feasts—Chuza would not come to his bed until well after midnight.

I cannot say that I greatly missed Chuza's daily visits, but his constant anxiety was a trial. Soon I was feeling stress. He could neither keep still nor sleep at night. What slight affection Herod held for him was soon eroded by Herod's new wife, who disliked Chuza. My husband would twist and turn in our bed, repeating gossip he heard, terrified that it might be true.

"Today, I overheard her maid saying that she called me, 'Rat face.' The maid told me that Herod's wife suspected me of stealing from the kitchen coffers!" My anguished husband groaned late one night as he paced through our rooms making it impossible for me to sleep. "I, who have never taken anything beyond my portion nor stolen even a mite! Why does she say such things?"

To torture you, I answered silently, but to comfort him I said aloud, "It is idle gossip, Chuza. The maid making a game of you. Ignore it, for everyone knows you are no thief." This was true. Whatever one might say about Chuza, he was grateful for his position in Herod's court. He would never consider taking anything beyond the portion allotted to us. Herod had been generous, and we had no need for more.

Soon that changed. The false queen set her malicious sights upon my poor husband, and because the very sight of him seemed to displease her, she took pleasure in making his life miserable. Our portion was reduced. We found that we had less food and fewer things to wear than even the minor slaves at court have.

We did have enough to survive, though. When Chuza complained bitterly about the reduction in our circumstances, I cautioned him, "It is not as though we are reduced to begging. Herod will never turn you out, no matter what authority over you he seems to give his wife. He would not do that to you." But my husband was not satisfied. He believed that if he could only find a way to win the false queen's favor, all would be well again. I had not the heart to tell him that his face and cringing demeanor already defeated him.

One morning he woke me at dawn; he had come in so late I had not heard him. "I know how to earn the queen's favor," he said excitedly as I struggled to stay awake. When I lit a lamp, I saw that his eyes were feverish and wide, and I swallowed my irritation. Without waiting for me to ask, he said, "The queen recently had John, the one they call the Baptist, arrested and thrown into Herod's dungeons. She is not satisfied. She silenced John's criticisms of her marriage to Herod, but now she has turned her sights to the Baptist's cousin, Jesus, a preacher and prophet whom John claims is the Messiah. She is now worried that Jesus will take up the cry against her where John left off."

"And what has this to do with us?" I asked, my annoyance finally surfacing. The sun had not begun to rise, and I wanted to go back to sleep. His next words jolted me awake and robbed me of the slightest prospect of sleep. "You will spy on Jesus!"

My shriek was enough to make him put his hand over my mouth, and he rushed on before I could remove it. "Listen to me, Joanna! If you join those who follow Jesus, you can tell me his plans, and I can pass them on to the queen. In this way I would be useful, even necessary, to her. My former position would be restored. I might even be elevated."

"And just how am I to become a follower of this man?" I hissed in an outraged whisper. "Have you lost your mind for lack of sleep? Do you think it's so easy to become a disciple of this famous preacher?"

"It is!" he whispered back. "I have listened and learned. Jesus and his disciples accept anyone who chooses to follow him. They welcome strangers! Samaritans! Canaanites! Whores!"

"I thank you, husband, for putting me in such company," I interrupted dryly, but he was too frantic to notice and continued. "All you need do is go and listen to him. Mingle with the followers. They will accept you. Are you not always complaining of the lack of society here in the court? Following Jesus, you can see the wide world by day and return here by night to tell me what you discovered."

I was about to dismiss the idea as lunacy and go back to sleep, but then I looked at my husband, really looked at him. His eyes were sunken, the skin on his already thin face was taut, his expression haggard and exhausted. Yet now he was lit with excitement, a pathetic hope that had no foundation, and it made him piteous to look upon. He was, in his own way, a good man. He provided for me as well as he could. I realized that he desired his former position as much for my sake as his. While I looked into his face, he said with a breaking voice, "Please, wife. Please."

The next day Chuza made an arrangement to report to Herod's wife through her maid, the same one who repeated her cruel words. Herod's wife abruptly looked more kindly on my husband when she heard that he would bring her news of Jesus.

The following day, carrying money Chuza had hidden so that I would have something to offer the disciples, I set out to become a spy among the followers of Jesus. But I did not become a spy. Oh, it was easy enough to join them because they took his message of love and welcome to heart and were hospitable to new followers. I was accepted without question. A woman about my own age, Mary of Magdala, saw me standing aside from the group and took me by the arm to draw me in. She told me that Jesus had cured her of many illnesses and that all who heard him came to believe that he was the Messiah. She shared some food with me and invited me to stay with Jesus' followers for as long as I wished.

That first day nothing happened of note. I did not see anything to suggest that this man was the Messiah. He was at his leisure, seeming to enjoy himself. He was not serious like the Zealots who called for Rome's destruction. Jesus spoke to the people around him one by one. Although I didn't dare approach him that day, I could see that he comforted all who came to him. He also played with some children in the group (for many of the women who followed him also brought their children). His innocent delight in the little ones was so evident he might have been one of them himself. The children ate from his plate, and he waved away his disciples while he told the children stories.

My husband hardly believed me when I returned home with this report. He was waiting eagerly for me. As soon as I appeared he asked, "What then? Did he threaten Herod? Did he malign the queen as John did? Is he teaching revolution?"

"Revolution? He said nothing about Herod at all. Jesus seems not to know that the fox and his false queen even exist!" I was tired, and I felt as if I had been sent on a fool's errand. "There is nothing in this man that is threatening. He spent the day talking, eating, and playing with the children of his followers. Is this a man that Herod should fear?"

My husband was devastated. "But what shall I tell the queen?" He sounded sorry that Jesus was not a Zealot.

"Tell her what I told you!" I snapped. "Nothing!"

"The queen will never accept such news!" my husband squeaked, his voice high with fear. "She expects to hear how this man has incited the crowd against Herod and her and Rome. Jesus is the Baptist's cousin. He must be teaching the same dangerous doctrine that John taught!"

"And I tell you that he does not speak of violence or uprising!"

"You must go back!" Chuza insisted, undaunted by my anger. "You must go back and discover something about him that will please her or her fury toward me will be worse than before."

I ignored him and went to bed. But I could not sleep because he spent the night pacing through our quarters and muttering to himself. His fear was like a swarm of locusts filling the air. Finally, to give us both the chance to sleep, I told him, "One more day! I will join them one more day. If I see no more than I saw today, you can make something up to tell that malevolent hag!"

I wonder now if Chuza regrets sending me that next day. Everything changed. Jesus was traveling that day, teaching the crowd that accompanied him as he walked. A man called Jairus, who was a leader of the synagogue, rushed up to him and with tears and many gestures, begged Jesus to heal his small daughter who was near death. When Jesus embraced the man gently and agreed, I realized that there was much more to all this than the relaxed man I had seen yesterday. I went along and watched with great interest. The crowd had grown excited; it was clear they believed that Jesus could heal the child.

Before we reached Jairus' home, there was a disturbance in the throng around Jesus. I pushed forward to see what happened. An old woman was kneeling before Jesus, proclaiming that she had been healed of the hemorrhage that plagued her for years. The crowd was silent until Jesus helped her rise and then praised her faith. After that the people were more restive than ever, some praising him aloud as everyone continued toward Jairus' house. I turned to look at this old woman. She walked upright beside a young man who must have been her son. The look of inexpressible gratitude on her face took my breath away, and my doubts about her healing were dispelled. I turned and hurried to catch up with the others.

As we approached Jairus' house, a man came out to meet him, saying, "Your daughter is dead, do not trouble the teacher any longer." Upon hearing this, Jairus stumbled and fell to the ground. Jesus helped him up and said, "Do not fear. Only believe." There were people wailing about the girl's death and to them he said, "The child is not dead but sleeping." The people milling outside the house scorned him, but Jesus went in with Jairus, and with his disciples Peter, John, and James. When Jesus came out of the house the same people who scorned him were crying that the girl was well, that that he brought her back to life! I saw her myself because she came outside, a trembling, pale little thing, to bid Jesus a shy farewell.

It was time for me to return to Chuza, but I found it hard to leave Jesus and the disciples. After just two days, I felt I belonged more with these near strangers than I ever had in my parent's home or in Herod's palace with Chuza. But I knew Chuza would be more distressed than ever if I was late, so I broke away from the disciples. When I turned once to glance back, Jesus looked directly at me. I stopped abruptly and made a soft cry of surprise. I felt he knew who I was, what I came to do, and how I intended to betray him to Herod's wife. My heart seemed to stop as I fell from the heights of joy at being among his disciples to the depths of shame at being discovered. And then something astonishing happened: Jesus smiled at me. His face lit, his eyes seemed to encompass me, and I felt forgiven.

I have been a disciple since that day. I have long since traded the jewels from my dowry to support his work. I accompanied John's disciples when they told Jesus that Herod had beheaded John at the request of his stepdaughter and her evil mother. I saw him weep and turn away. And later, when he returned to us, I was able to tell him that John was true to him to the end, loudly proclaiming Jesus as the

Messiah from Herod's dungeons. I told of Herod's fear of him and about the plots against him, yet these reports did not affect Jesus.

My husband has accused me of betraying him, becoming a spy for the one I was sent to spy on. Perhaps he is right. I can't explain my feelings toward Chuza now. I pity him and, strangely, care more for him now that I have learned what it means to love. I still live with Chuza, although he is completely out of favor with Herod and his wife and is barely accepted in court. As Jesus grew in reputation and popularity, Herod became increasingly suspicious of everyone, from his leading counselor to the lowliest slave. My husband is no longer the exception. I tried to convince him to leave everything and join the disciples but he could not bring himself to release his vain hope of winning back his high place in the palace.

This morning Chuza protested vehemently when I told him what I planned to do today. I have gathered spices and oils. I am going on my way with Salome and Mary Magdalene and the other women, my sisters, to anoint Jesus' body. He has been in the tomb since the day before the Sabbath. I stood with the other women and with his mother and watched him die in agony. I held his mother in my arms when her body writhed as though struck with her son's pain. We will show our love and respect by preparing his body. Chuza said I would be the cause of his death as well as mine. What is that to me, who has died with my Lord? I will go to the tomb.

Active Meditation

All over the world, people like Joanna risk their lives for Jesus, spreading the gospel by bringing food, water, shelter, jobs, and hope to impoverished people. Many people are committed to Jesus and his teachings in ways that go well beyond what most of us can imagine.

You can help bring the good news to the poor. If your parish does not have a supportive relationship with a mission or missionary, try to establish one. Some parishes have "sister" cities in areas like Haiti and Africa. Others regularly support missionaries who visit the parish to conduct retreats or to report on their work. Suburban parishes can support the work of urban neighbors.

If your parish has a relationship with a missionary group, get involved. If not, encourage one or get involved yourself in a missionary-type ministry by giving money, exchanging information, and sending clothes and food to support Christ's work.

Reflection/Discussion Questions

1. When have you risked something important to you for your faith? Describe the event.

2. How would you describe the relationship between courage and faith?

3. Be a modern-day Joanna. Describe following Jesus today. What do you observe? What is Jesus doing? Saying? How does this affect you?

CHAPTER IX

Martha and Mary

Prophets, Disciples, Friends

LUKE 10:38–42 AND JOHN 11:1—12:9–11

I cast myself onto the ground in grief over the death our brother, Lazarus. As I look up from the floor, I see my sister, Martha, standing in the doorway. She draws me to my feet, and says, "The teacher is here and is calling for you." With my sudden, fresh tears comes a flood of memories.

Jesus had long been a friend with Lazarus, Martha, and me. It was not unusual for Jesus to bring his followers to our home. Jesus used our large estate in Bethany as a frequent stopping place as he traveled. Bethany was only a short distance from Jerusalem, and Jesus was often with us, especially during Passover and the other festivals.

I remember a time Jesus visited us, a much happier time, in the early days of his work. He came to stay with us, and he brought along some of his disciples. Lazarus greeted him joyfully and welcomed his followers, Martha pulled me aside. "We must prepare food and rooms for all of them!" she whispered. "It is our duty as Lazarus' sisters to show them hospitality. Come and help me!"

As usual my sister overreacted. She worried about everything, from whether the fish for dinner was fresh enough to serve, to the proper time for sowing the seeds in our garden. Lazarus and I often teased her about this tendency. She would always respond, with a little hurt in her righteous voice, "It is fine to criticize me, but I don't hear either of you complaining about your easy lifestyle or the good food I put before you both every day. I don't hear you asking how your bedding became so clean and fresh or how water appeared for your bathing!" And she was right. To be fair, Martha worked constantly to be sure we were comfortable. She made our household, with its many guests and visitors, a pleasant, welcoming place. This was no easy task, and we often failed to give her proper credit for her work.

That day when Jesus came to us, I put off her request for help. I told her, "Let me sit awhile with Jesus, and then I'll come to help you." She rolled her eyes and blew out a sigh as if to say, "I've heard that before," but she had too much on her mind to bother arguing with me. She disappeared into the inner rooms while I sat by Jesus, Lazarus, and the rest of the disciples. I loved to listen to Jesus, even before he became known for his preaching. His voice was beautiful, and I usually understood the meaning of his preaching. The rabbis and scribes simply confused me.

When Jesus spoke of the Father, I felt he knew the Father. I think Jesus could bring the Father to me. When Jesus explained the prophets and Scripture, I knew he understood the prophets and Scripture in a way that no ordinary teacher could understand them. And his voice had a quality to it that I could never explain, but listening to him I felt all my anxieties and sorrows fall away. Lazarus and I had often discussed this unusual feeling, for my brother experienced the same thing. We both told Martha more than once that it would do her some good to spend more time listening to Jesus than cooking and cleaning for him. She would just give us both "the look," and go back to whatever she was doing.

On this particular evening Jesus was recounting for us how earlier that day a young lawyer had questioned him on what was necessary to attain eternal life. Jesus, in turn, had asked the lawyer to name what he thought were the most important commandments. The lawyer, wisely, had answered, "You shall love the Lord your God with all your heart, and with all your soul, and with all your strength, and with all your mind; and your neighbor as yourself." Jesus, pleased with his answer, had been ready to dismiss him, but the lawyer asked Jesus, "Who is my neighbor?"

Jesus said that he knew the man might well have been sent to test him, so he told the lawyer a parable about a Jew who had been beaten, stripped, robbed, and left by the side of the road. Jesus said that in the story a priest and then a Levite passed by the injured man. Then a Samaritan (who everyone knows is despised) cleansed the man's wounds and lifted him onto his own mule. The Samaritan then brought the wounded man to an inn where he left money for the innkeeper to continue to care for him, promising more money when he returned. Upon finishing the tale, Jesus said he asked the lawyer, "Which of these three, do you think, was a neighbor to the man who fell into the hands of the robbers?" Of course it was the Samaritan, and the lawyer willingly acknowledged this. Once again, I marveled at how Jesus could explain a precept so simply and clearly and at the same time challenge our beliefs and traditions.

Unfortunately Martha had not heard a word of Jesus' story. She was busy the whole time Jesus was talking, moving rapidly through the rooms. I could sense her irritation in the very air. I knew she wanted my help, but it was hard for me to leave Jesus. His visits were less frequent now because his preaching and healing ministry had expanded. I was loathe to miss any opportunity to hear him. Besides, I didn't see why Lazarus should be the only one to enjoy Jesus and his disciples. Finally, when my sister could no longer contain herself, she burst in. Ignoring me and Lazarus, she strode right up to Jesus.

"Lord, do you not care that my sister has left me to do all the work by myself? Tell her then to help me."

Jesus looked at her mildly and took her hand so as to soften what he was about to say. "Martha, Martha, you are worried and distracted by many things; there is need of only one thing. Mary has chosen the better part, which will not be taken away from her."

My sister looked as though someone had slapped her. I immediately felt sorry for her and for my lack of compassion in refusing to help her. Still I knew that Jesus was right; Lazarus and I had been telling her to relax and embrace whatever opportunity we had to spend time with him. She never fully understood what a gift was offered to her in the simple fact of his presence. Now I watched her respond to Jesus' words. He kept his hand on hers to alleviate the sting of his words. Lazarus and I exchanged glances; much as we wanted her to spend more time with Jesus, we did not wish to see her in pain. My brother and I were both painfully aware that we did not help her enough in our home. But perhaps because Jesus remained near her, the stunned hurt that came over her face passed away as she looked into Jesus' eyes. A spark of understanding flared in my sister's intelligent eyes, and she lowered herself gracefully to sit by Jesus and listen to the rest of his words.

I remembered that early visit now as Martha, my sturdy, dependable sister holds me upright and tells me that Jesus is coming. It is hard for me not to feel that Jesus is coming too late. At the first sign of my brother's sickness, we had not been afraid; Lazarus was a hearty man and strong. He acted as if the sickness was something that would pass soon, more fatigue than anything else. Of course it would pass, we thought. Slowly the disease seemed to root itself in his very core, destroying him little by little. Eventually my brother became exhausted and in terrible pain.

We sent word to Jesus, who was teaching across the Jordan. It was a simple message, "Lord, he whom you love is ill." We were certain that he would come immediately to see Lazarus. We knew by now that our beloved friend had the power to heal, and we believed that he would heal Lazarus, no matter how far the malady had progressed. Martha and I were surprised, and then hopeful, when our messenger returned reporting that Jesus had responded by saying, "This illness does not lead to death; rather it is for God's glory, so that the Son of God may be glorified through it." At first, we wondered at this answer, but as we thought about it we took hope. We knew that Jesus could heal even from a great distance. We expected my brother to get well.

Shortly after Jesus' answer arrived, our brother died.

And yet at this very moment, Jesus is just outside the village waiting for me. Lazarus has been in the tomb for four days. Martha goes to meet Jesus while I stay home. Our home is filled with guests, although these guests came to help us mourn our brother. It seems that Jerusalem must be empty, there are so many people with us. Lazarus had more friends than any ten men together, and all grieve for him and for us. The one friend who might have saved him has finally come.

As I prepare to greet Jesus, Martha describes the conversation she has already had with him about Lazarus. She told me that when she saw him she said, "Lord, if you had been here, my brother would not have died. But even now I know that God will give you whatever you ask of him." Martha told me that Jesus answered her, "Your brother will rise again." She said that she told Jesus, "I know that he will rise again in the resurrection on the last day."

At this, Martha says that Jesus said her, "I am the resurrection and the life. Those who believe in me, even though they die, will live, and everyone who lives and believes in me will never die. Do you believe this?"

My sister, who is bold and honest at all times, told me she answered, "Yes, Lord, I believe that you are the Messiah, the Son of God, the one coming into the world." Martha and I looked into each other's eyes. We had often discussed among the three of us whether Jesus was the Messiah. Of course we knew that he taught and preached in Judea and Galilee and that he even went to the Samaritans, the Canaanites, and other foreigners. His outreach to the Gentiles was this sort of thing that infuriated some of the Pharisees and scribes. Everyone knew that we were his friends; he trusted us to feed and house him and his disciples. We shared many long conversations with him about Scripture and the prophets, but we never asked him if he was the Messiah, and he never named himself "Messiah" in our home. We did wonder, though, especially as the numerous reports of his miracles reached us.

I think we were somewhat blinded by our closeness. After all, Jesus was our good friend. It is all but impossible to imagine that your closest friend, the one you laughed and eaten and wept and talked and joked with, is the Messiah of God. Our people expected the Messiah to astound the world, to be the awe-inspiring embodiment of God among us, to be the face of power who would move us to our destiny. It was difficult to think of this gentle friend as the one from God.

Now my sister confessed him to be the Messiah, and he had acknowledged it. What did this mean for us? What did it mean for Lazarus? She embraced me hard and then followed more slowly as I ran to meet Jesus.

The crowd, who are with us in our house and at the tomb, follow me. They do not know where I am going, or even that Jesus is approaching. I meet Jesus where Martha had left him and fall to my knees, crying, "Lord, if you had been here, my brother would not have died." I could not hold back my tears. Jesus says nothing, but he looks at me and those with us who are also weeping and wailing in their grief. He bends a little at the waist, swaying and groaning softly, as if deeply pained by a great burden.

"Where have you laid him?" is all he asks, barely above a whisper.

"Lord, come and see," they answer and then Jesus weeps.

Seeing Jesus weep, the people around us begin to murmur. While some took Jesus' tears as a sign of his great love for Lazarus, the more cynical among them observe that Jesus had performed many miracles, so why had he not saved my brother, whom he loved? Ignoring them, we walk to the tomb. Martha is now with us. Jesus studies the sealed cave where Lazarus lay and then commands, "Take away the stone." Martha says, "Lord, already there is a stench because he has been dead for four days."

Jesus, his attention still fixed on the tomb, replies, "Did I not tell you that if you believed, you would see the glory of God?"

Martha nods to some men in the group, and they remove the stone. By now my eyes are drawn to the open cave. Jesus looks toward heaven and calls out, "Father, I thank you for having heard me. I knew that you always hear me, but I have said this for the sake of the crowd standing here, so that they may believe that you sent me." Then after a short silence, he says, "Lazarus, come out!"

Martha's hand grips mine. Neither of us can breathe. I feel the beat of her blood racing like mine. The dark hole of the cave's entrance seems to shimmer and move. My brother, still wrapped in the funeral cloths, stumbles over the threshold and out into the light. My sister and I race forward with our first in-drawn breath, and fall upon him. We rip away his bindings and run our hands over him as if he is our long-lost child.

After we embrace Jesus and cling to Lazarus to our heart's content, I recover myself enough to notice that Jesus is quiet and withdrawn. Normally our discussions with Jesus around the table in our home were lively, but today he is mostly silent. The truth is that my sister and I and our jubilant guests are talking so rapidly and joyfully to Lazarus that Jesus could not have spoken even if he wished. It was obvious to me that Jesus has no more to say. He sits at Lazarus' side, hardly touching the abundant food people set before us.

Eventually the crowd begins to disperse. There is a group of prominent Jews from Jerusalem, the same ones who had muttered that Jesus should have healed Lazarus, who watch our tumultuous celebration. Although they are as astounded as the rest of us when Jesus raised my brother, they do not seem to share so fully in our rejoicing. Now these men slip out without bidding us farewell. Jesus, who seemed to take no notice of anything, rises to follow them.

Martha and I exchange glances. I realize that she noticed Jesus' silence and apparent weariness also. It is almost as if Jesus is spent and saddened by the day's events. Martha inclines her head toward the doorway where Jesus departed, and I know she wants me to follow him and see if all is well. I feel suddenly shy, as if the man who has been my dearest friend is now a stranger whom I dare not approach. But I shake off this foolishness, telling myself that if Jesus needs consoling, it is the least I can do. I walk into the cooling twilight where he stands gazing after the men walking back to Jerusalem close together in conversation.

I move quietly to Jesus' side and slip my arm into his. "Lord," I whisper, "What is it? What troubles you on this glorious night?"

A soft, wistful smile, unlike the grin I had grown to love, slowly forms on his face, although he does not turn to look at me. He tightens my arm comfortingly in his own and clasps my hand. After a while, he nods toward the fading group, "Where do you think those men are going, Mary?"

"Why, home to Jerusalem, Lord," I reply, puzzled at the gravity of his question.

"Yes." he nods. "Home to Jerusalem. Home to the chief priests to give their evidence. And so it begins."

Active Meditation

"Mary has chosen the better part." It is good to be like Mary, who ignored everything to pay attention to Jesus. It is also fair to say that Christianity would not have flourished and spread without the "Marthas" of the world, those believers who are active and serve the needs of the church and the community. Are you more like Martha or Mary? If you are more like Mary, i.e., committed to prayer and contemplation, add an active component to your faith: help prepare a meal for a soup kitchen, serve on a church council or committee, or volunteer in some other way. If you are more like Martha, active and busy, take some time to simply be with Jesus: meditate, pray, read the gospels and other books about Jesus, and spend quiet time in church or another sacred space.

Reflection/Discussion Questions

1. How do you think Martha felt when Jesus answered her request to make Mary help her? When have you felt embarrassed for doing something you thought was right?

2. Do you believe that one sister demonstrated a stronger faith than the other did? If so, which sister and why?

3. The only time any gospel states directly that Jesus wept was when he stood outside Lazarus' tomb. Why do you think Jesus wept? Comment on Jesus' humanity.

CHAPTER X

The Adulteress

Disciple of Justice and Forgiveness

JOHN 8:1–11

I had not yet risen from the bed when a horde of men burst into the room, shouting and cursing in their violence, laying their hands on me, bruising me, twisting my limbs, their lustful cruelty more brutal than anything I had ever known. This was only the beginning.

They found me with a man in a small room he keeps for us on the outskirts of Jerusalem where he does business. This man, who is not my husband, has another home for his family some distance away. He never speaks of his wife and children, although I know that his other home is opulent. His father-in-law gave it to him as a part of his wife's dowry, along with a high place in the family's trading business.

With this man, I never speak of my husband or my long dreary days in our lonely house. I never share that I long for a child or that I secretly hope that he will give me a child (for my husband cannot). I say nothing about my husband's disgust with me, or my bruises or how he blamed me for not bearing him a son. On the day the men rushed in, this man and I were desperate lovers who very carefully selected our topics of conversation.

We were taken just after we fell into a half-wakeful slumber. We are never fully relaxed when we are together. We always knew that we had to part by the noon sun and did not have the time for a meal together. In seven months we shared a mere three meals and only partial nights. We will not eat together today. The men who broke violently into the room will see to that. Shouting triumphantly, they take hold of me, tearing at my scanty robe, dragging me into the street where the well-primed mob awaits.

My lover protests until one of them shoves him to the floor, snarling, "Hold your peace and we'll spare you, fool! We have no use for you. You can well afford to lose this little whore, but can you afford to lose your life? Eh? Are you so wealthy that the stones won't crush and cut you? Or will your wife and her rich parents be well pleased to hear of this squalid room? Are you anxious to have your name published through the region, a lying adulterer, taken in the act? Will your young sons be proud?" Laughing nastily, he watches my lover avert his eyes, shamed and weakened.

I do not blame him. I recognize some of these men. They are the servants and parasites who make their living cringing before the Temple leaders, ever ready to do their bidding and capable of anything. They will think nothing of killing him here or of destroying his family. I have seen these ruffians hanging about the crowds wherever the preacher Jesus speaks.

Jesus is in the region, teaching in the temple. The few times I have seen him, these men were slinking in the background, their faces sour, their attitude full of scorn as though consumed by envy for the attention Jesus so easily attracted. I know by the way they handle me and sneer at my lover that they are jealous of him as well; few of them have the means to keep a family as well as a young mistress in another city. When they pull me out into the street, they leave him behind. The last thing I hear from my lover is a wrenching sob.

Humiliation and rage war within me as I am paraded through the streets, struck and spit upon, wearing no more than my sheer, torn robe. I cannot help but see the people who line the paths, some rushing from their homes to drink in my shame with deep pleasure. I live in this place and not a few of the people know me. My neighbors have despised me from the moment my husband brought me home as his new bride two years ago. He rejected a local girl in favor of me; most here have never forgiven me. I know how swiftly the news will be brought to my husband, a tenant farmer in an olive grove to the south.

How delightful it will be for the neighbor who manages to reach him first. I imagine it will be the father of the rejected girl, who still mopes about her parents' house, unmarried. How pleased he will be to see my husband's initial look turn from one of concern at the thought that something happened to me to anguished disbelief when he learns the news. There will be the inevitable anger, and then that neighbor will see the face that I have so often seen, the face my husband cannot control, the face that destroys all memory of his other, kinder, calmer faces. This neighbor, who has abhorred me for what he thinks of as my airs, has no idea what happens behind the door of my house. He has no idea what his favored daughter was spared.

My fellow villagers hurry out to watch me pass. I see the smug satisfaction on the faces of the women, the older, unattractive ones who hate anything fresh or pretty or young. I see the leers on the faces of their husbands, whose eyes gleam with lewd pleasure at having their fantasies affirmed. Even children are encouraged to watch my mortification, though their mothers keep a tight hold on them, making sure they don't come close enough to be contaminated.

I recognize one small girl from my neighborhood, a young cousin of the family who holds me accountable for their daughter's unmarried state. This child, though, always offered me a quiet, courteous greeting whenever our paths cross. I think of her as my ally, if a mere child can be such a thing. She recognizes me and starts forward, a look of confused horror on her face as if to ask me, "What has happened to you?" I imagine her thin arms around my neck, comforting me, drawing me out of this nightmare. She raises a small, pale hand and tries to break free of her mother, who yanks her back and slaps her hard across the face. I flinch as I realize that I managed to hurt the only one in this crowd who cares about me.

In the blur of cruelty all around me, I catch glimpses of something I do not expect to see. There are younger women who have fear in their wide eyes as they follow me. I am moved at what I take as their compassion, but then I realize they are not afraid for me. They fear the power of this mob, the power of men who can turn against a woman and do what they will with her. These few, frightened women will remember this moment long into their lives.

Bitterness consumes me. These hypocrites! These men who come at the bidding of their Pharisee masters and these neighbors who watch with such malevolent glee. What do they come to see? Am I worse than our revered King David, who had a woman's husband killed so that he might possess her? No, and yet he is continually honored by the same leaders who revel in my shame. Am I worse than his son, Solomon, who had palaces crowded with wives and concubines and still turned to foreigners because the women of Israel were not enough for him? No, and yet the scribes and lawyers cite Solomon for his wisdom and brilliance. And what of our father, Abraham, who forced a slave girl to take his seed and bear his son, only to banish her and her son to what would have been a slow death in the desert, was it not for God's mercy? Where is the mercy in these men and this crowd?

Abruptly all thoughts of these revered kings and founders are driven away along with all hope for mercy when a tall, heavily-built man in the mob raises his fist. He brandishes a rock and shouts, "Stone the adulteress!" To me he screams, "You will die for playing the whore!"

I stumble, my legs made weak and useless, until the Pharisees' men yank me up again. As the full import of my situation takes hold, all emotion is eclipsed by pure, gut-twisting terror.

I will be stoned.

Our law allows stoning, and stoning is what these men and their masters intend. My lover has escaped for some reason, perhaps because of his power and money; that protection does not extend to me. Though I knew the law and must have been aware that this could happen, I never believed it in my heart. I never really considered stoning as a possibility. In fact, this punishment is not often imposed. The priests and rabbis often choose to let husbands resolve such issues in private. But today there will be no private resolution. Why have they chosen me? Of all women, why me and why now? My lover and I have met for months. My captors drag me along, now faint with fear. I am covered with cuts, burns, and filth from the road.

Jesus sees me battered and broken when they fling me at his feet where he is seated, teaching in the Temple: a bleeding, bedraggled, filthy girl, half-naked, unable to even lift her head for pain, fear, and humiliation. I am profoundly ashamed now, for I know well who Jesus is, though I wonder why the crowd brought me before him instead of the Pharisees. These thugs do not work for Jesus; many would say they work for his enemies. Jesus is a teacher, a healer, and a man known for his kindness to women, certainly not a judge of Israel. And Jesus has no power over me, so why have they dropped me here?

With that question comes a glimmer of an awful truth, increasing my shame and sorrow; the masters of this vicious mob intended all along to use me to trap Jesus. How long had they observed me from the shadows, waiting for this perfect moment? How long had they waited, watching our trysts, waiting because it was not yet the opportune time to discredit Jesus? How long had they anticipated this particular day when Jesus would be teaching in the temple, surrounded by his followers and those who wanted to believe in him? They had failed so often in the past to destroy him, but because of me they will succeed this time. Oh, I will still be stoned, of that I have no doubt, but I will first be used as a stone cast against Jesus. And not just a stone, but a crushing boulder.

After I am cast in the dirt before Jesus, there is a long moment of silence. I can hear some of my tormentors breathing heavily in triumphant exertion, but even their gasps gradually subside. Jesus makes no move, and I lay still as death. Finally a short, wizened Pharisee, who is known for displaying his piousness and always appearing early at the Temple on feast days, and some scribes come forward to speak.

"Teacher," they say with subtle sarcasm, "this woman was caught in the very act of committing adultery. Now in the law Moses commanded us to stone such women. Now what do you say?"

The silence lengthens until it becomes unbearable. I am unable to raise my face to Jesus, so fraught am I with terror and self-loathing. I hear a few rough whispers and then Jesus' robe rustling as he bends over me, as if protecting me with his body. The whispers become murmurs as he gently rearranges my tattered robe, covering my nakedness. Tears of weakness and gratitude escape my closed eyelids, and his touch calms me as I sense that he shares my anguish. Without answering the Pharisee or straightening up, he begins to write with his finger on the ground.

Time passes in this strange tableau, the mob growing more agitated by the moment. Those who had come to hear Jesus were pushed into the background, where they mill about. They are anxious about what will happen. How will their teacher escape this trap? Finally the exasperated Pharisee loudly repeats the deceitful query, "Well, what of it? Are we to stone her?"

I tremble at the words and their volume, but there is no tremor in Jesus as he slowly rises to his feet and regards the crowd. After gazing in turn at each of those gathered, he says simply, "Let anyone among you who is without sin be the first to throw a stone at her." Immediately, he leans back over me and begins writing again on the ground.

The words echo in the charged silence. I am horrified at his challenge, certain I will now die in a hail of rocks. I only comprehend his wisdom as moments pass and nothing happens. But when I hear someone scurry about to find a rock, I flinch and prepare for the first strike.

Jesus does not stir, but stays close to me. I lack his complete faith and can all but feel a rock splitting my skin, breaking a bone. Pressing my face into the ground, as if I could crawl into the earth and be hidden forever, I can taste the dirt mix with the blood in my mouth. I glance in the direction of the neighbor who still mutters, enraged. Before he can heave the sizable rock he clutches, one of the elders stops him, firmly grasping his arm. Together, they move away from the increasingly confused crowd. As I watch openly now, amazed, they all begin to retreat, singly or in pairs.

Despite the relief that floods my body, I notice the piercing looks of hatred the leaders and their men have for Jesus. The Pharisees and scribes who spoke look at him like vipers that haved missed their chance to strike. Jesus has made certain that I will live through this day.

In the dark days to come, I will wonder if I had caused Jesus to take one step closer to his death. In turning the tables on the vengeful crowd, he has swollen their ever-growing reservoir of hatred that would eventually engulf and destroy him. I would realize this much later; Jesus himself now seems undisturbed by what has happened. He ignored the departure of his enemies the way he ignored their presence. Even as Jesus' followers withdraw to eagerly discuss the meaning of this confrontation, Jesus continues to write on the ground. He does so until my last accuser has gone. They have no interest in me, but then they never truly did, as I now clearly see.

Jesus stops tracing in the dirt. He rises and brings me to my feet. I still cannot meet his eyes. As if understanding my shame, he does not force me to look at him when he asks, "Woman, where are they? Has no one condemned you?"

Barely able to hear my own voice, I whisper, "No one, sir."

In that voice that lodges in my heart as much as my mind, he says, "Neither do I condemn you. Go your way, and from now on, do not sin again."

My body and my soul thrill to his words. Never before, not with my husband, not with my lover, have I felt this way. How will I ever deserve the tenderness with which he treated me? Is it possible for me to change my heart so completely? How can I feel so pure after the life I have lived? Am I worthy to live the life he restored to me? How will I do it? If he has forgiven me, can I forgive myself?

My emotions plunge me into chaos, yet when Jesus walks away from me, I know I will follow. Sooner or later. Where else would I go now?

Active Meditation

The New Testament is filled with stories of redemption. Forgiveness is implied in redemption. The adulteress is forgiven and redeemed by being given the chance to change. Is there some behavior fir which you have sought and received the Lord's forgiveness and redemption? List the sins that Jesus has forgiven you and from which he has redeemed you. Give thanks for each incident and ask Jesus to continue healing you. Then list those occasions that you know have tempted you in the past and perhaps resulted in sin, occasions that are likely to rise again. Pray daily over this list, selecting one each day, praying for the courage and wisdom to remain focused on living as a disciple of Jesus. Ask yourself what concrete steps you can take to minimize the danger of sinning.

Reflection/Discussion Questions

1. According to Mosaic Law, anyone caught in adultery could be stoned. Why do you think the Jewish leaders brought only the woman, and not the man, before Jesus?

2. Do you think men who have affairs are blamed less harshly than women? Why or why not?

3. When Jesus bent down to write in the sand, what do you think he was writing or illustrating?

CHAPTER XI

Pilate's Wife

Frightened Prophet

MATTHEW 27:11–19

I toss and turn in the wringing heat of this desolate place, my bed-clothes drenched in sweat. I yearn for the comforts and safety of Rome. I am plagued by questions and sleep poorly—when I sleep at all. Why was my husband sent to govern Judea, this uncivilized out-post, this land of strange religions and people who claim there is only one God? Is this a punishment from Caesar or a challenge? Was Pontius sent here because, as his admirers have said, only someone with his clever skills could bring order to this chaotic place? That only he could crush the Zealots who defy Rome with their bloody revolts? Or are we are here, as my husband's enemies claim, because he is certain to fail since no one can govern this region? Do his ene-mies want him to be disgraced before Caesar and all of Rome? If my husband does well, will we return to Rome with great honor and be given a desirable place in Caesar's empire? If he fails, what will become of us? Will Pontius become a mere soldier, only to be killed defending the empire in some brutal skirmish?

Who can answer these questions? Surely no one here in Jerusalem, a city full of men and women who would just as soon knife my husband in the back as share a goblet of wine with him. There is treachery all around us. There is that greedy, deceitful Herod, who calls himself king, in disdain of Caesar. There are the Pharisees and high priests, who nod to Pontius' face and plot behind his back. And of course there are the Zealots who wage open war on Rome, not to mention the shepherds and farmers who slyly withhold taxes from the empire. All would be pleased to see my husband gone as a failure or murdered in his sleep. Not a few would be happy to kill him.

I worry about him constantly, although he prefers that I do not bring these concerns to him. He has enough of his own. I knew from the moment we arrived that Herod and his so-called wife, this "queen" who was once the wife of Herod's brother, would be dangerous to us. As if Herod is not bad enough, with his sharp envy of anyone who might usurp his power (and by our very presence here, Pontius is on the top of his list). That woman is a malevolent force by herself. With her bizarre headdress, lavish clothes, and braids of jewels, I could see her scornfully dismiss me with a glance at the feast Herod gave in our honor when we first arrived. It was not to honor Pontius but to examine both him and me for any weakness or vulnerability that might be exploited. Once this woman decided to ignore me, her eyes never left my husband, and I realized she was more of a threat than Herod was.

Herod's palace is filled with excess, unlike this stark place to which we are assigned. Oh, I brought what comforts I could, as well as my own servants, but nothing Rome provides us here can possibly compare with the elaborate riches of Herod's palace. The palace has flawless woven rugs and tapestries, silk drapes in drenching colors that hang everywhere, priceless tiles, and carvings, gems, and gold throughout. Even the water vessels are costly. And these foolish Jews complain about paying taxes to Caesar? Who pays for the wealth that surrounds Herod and his queen?

One of my women, a trusted servant who came with me from my father's house, tells me that this queen has come with a gift for me. She did not send first to find if she would be welcome, or if I was prepared to receive her. No. She simply comes in full regalia, as if to ambush me. I am not dressed; what reason is there for me to dress in this miserable heat? There are no women here for me to associate with besides my slaves (although they are good servants, they are not companions). How I long for my sister and friends in Rome, our afternoons spent gossiping about who would rise and fall from power in the next election, the long, wine-loosened dinners where we could judge the way of things just by noting who sat where and who spoke with whom. Here there is no one of my class or religion to share even a simple meal, much less to exchange confidences.

And how can I expect my servants to make up for what I left behind in Rome? Besides, they silently resent this duty in Judea, perhaps more than I do; they were forced to come, but I chose to accompany my husband. My decision sentenced them to the prison of this land after they enjoyed the relative freedom as the highborn servants in a Roman leader's household. But what else could I do? Allow Pontius to come to his desperate land alone and without any assistance? Take my leisure in Rome while he suffered and put himself at risk in this den of wolves? Pontius and I are not unusual in Rome; like many couples, we were wed in a political match and our marriage has been focused on his career and the advancement of the empire. Where we differ is that we have both come to love and respect each other, a situation that is found infrequently in Rome. Pontius always listens to me as he might any political advisor, and he values me for much more than my well-connected family. I would never advise him publicly, but when we are alone, he asks my opinion and I give it freely. Such is our union. I never considered leaving him to confront this fate alone.

I think of all this as I hurriedly dress to meet the viper who calls herself Herod's wife. Even my best robe will seem bland next to her garish raiment, but I care little for this woman's opinion, except in how it may affect my husband. I go out and greet her coolly, hoping my dismay at her presence is not evident. She smiles, as if at some private joke, and thrusts forward a small, thin girl, dressed in a rough, dun-colored robe. The child's face is bruised on one side, and her dark eyes burn. She deliberately pulls away from Herod's wife, and I see the woman's composure crack for a moment; a disturbed look passes over her face. She has to deliberately lower the hand that has risen to strike the girl. The child smiles in bleak triumph.

The queen says, "My husband and I wish to show our utmost respect for the wife of our governor. Thus, we bring you this gift: your own Hebrew slave. This girl will serve you well in ways your servants may not know in our land."

Shocked, I cannot think of how to reply. I see that my servants, who just joined me, are aghast at the thought of this dirty creature before them joining their ranks. My mind races: do I dare offend Herod by refusing this "gift"? I have no need of the child and besides, I am certain she is meant to be a spy for Herod in my home. I flinch at the thought of her living with us, yet I cannot form an appropriately respectful rejection. The queen, taking great pleasure in my confusion, widens her smile, nods as though she has had something vital confirmed. She turns to go, leaving the child in my courtyard. I must do something.

I open my mouth to protest that I cannot accept such a priceless gift but at the moment, the girl hurls herself forward and falls at my feet. She hooks her arms around my ankles, and holds me tight, as if to keep me from following Herod's woman. I see her upturned face covered with tears. Her raw plea is in her eyes, and the run over the bruises on her face. I look up and watch the queen lifted into her heavily draped conveyance and depart.

The child will not let go even after the sounds of departure fade. My maids look horrified and finally step forward to pull her off me. I hold up my hand, and when they halt, surprised, I say only, "Leave us." My personal servant, Katera, gives the child a mean look, but I ignore it. When the child and I are alone, I bend over and say softly, "Stand up. No one will harm you here."

The little girl releases me and slowly gets to her feet. She will not look at me, fearing perhaps that I might still dismiss her. "What is your name?" I ask gently, wondering what it is about this girl that touches my heart.

"Lia." She says no more, her eyes still averted. I continue, "How old are you, Lia?"

"That woman says that I am eleven, but she lies. She took me from my parents for a small purse of money when I was just a baby. She has told me nothing of my family, other than that I am so wretched that my parents did not want me."

"What happened to your face?" I ask in the same quiet voice. When she presses her lips together and refuses to answer, I say more sternly, "Come now, you heard the queen. You belong to me now, and must do as I say. Unless you wish to be sent back to Herod's…"

She looks up at me quickly with questioning fear. Being reassured by what she sees in my face, she finally says with a bitterness far beyond her years, "Do not call that woman a 'queen,' for she is no queen! We have had no real queen since Esther. You, lady, are more queen than she!" I smile, knowing she is flattering me, but sensing a depth in her anger that might prove useful. "Tell me," I insist, "what happened to your face?"

Her lips tremble a little, but she finally answers, "I was punished."

As if I didn't know that, I think to myself, trying to be patient. "Why were you punished?"

This time the silence is longer. She seems to be considering whether her transgression will make me reject her. Knowing she has no choice, she says, "She beat me because I used to visit the Baptist in the dungeons before she had him killed. I brought him food and listened to him talk about Jesus."

She speaks a language I hardly comprehend. These people and their beliefs! Who can follow it all? There had been a scandal over a ragged preacher in Herod's dungeon, a man imprisoned because he claimed that the Messiah had come and because he harangued Herod about taking his brother's wife. This man was beheaded at the request of the queen and her seductive, vicious daughter, whom I met at the feast given in our honor. And Jesus? I knew little of this one, except that he was making life difficult for the leaders. They continually complain about him to Pontius.

Lia watches me with cautious eyes, as if still worried I might send her back. To calm her, I ask, "Why did you risk a beating to go to this man?"

Her look is incredulous. "Because he knew the Messiah! Because he told me about Jesus!"

"Why do you call Jesus Messiah?" I ask, curious about this man who drives the Jews to such distraction. Lia stares as if I have lost my senses. I am first amused and then disconcerted to see her pity at my evident ignorance. She grasps my wrist in excitement, not knowing that a slave could be flogged for such familiarity, and says, "John the Baptist told me about the miracles Jesus performed, of his teaching and kindness. And John would know; he was Jesus' cousin!"

It is easy to imagine what it must have meant to this girl, with no family at all, to hear a man talk with such love and admiration for his cousin. Of course, she had believed him. I decide to leave this subject, but I have one more question. "Lia," I ask somberly, "have you been sent to me as a spy for Herod and his woman?"

She now grips my arm harder. Her eyes widen, and then, to my surprise, she begins to grin. "Lady!" she laughs. "Is that what you think? She gave me to you because she hopes I will trouble you with my errant ways and drive you mad with my talk of John and Jesus! But spy? Never! She knows I would lie to her in every report! I hate her, and she knows better than to trust me."

Her vehemence satisfies me, and I tell her she may stay. Before she can abandon all propriety and throw her arms around me in gratitude, I call for Katera. "Find her a bed and clothes," I say with a stern look to make certain she understands that Lia is not to be ill-treated. I will not have jealousy among my servants. Still Katera asks resentfully, "And how shall this child serve?"

"At my pleasure," I snap, and Katera, chastised, leads Lia out.

At dinner I discuss my unusual day with Pontius, but he is distracted by the rumors he's heard of more unrest in the region. When I mention Lia's talk of Jesus, he is suddenly attentive. The subject that I was so ready to dismiss with the girl is of central importance to him.

"This man has all of Judea in turmoil," he explains. "Most of the Pharisees and Sadducees despise and even fear him because the common people love to listen to him. They flock by the thousands to remote coasts and mountainsides just to listen to him preach. Some even say that he feeds these thousands just by blessing a few loaves and fishes that then multiply, but of course that is foolishness. These people will believe anything! And so he's Rome's problem. The leaders are losing control. They fear that if Jesus calls for a revolution, he will have more followers than even the Zealots."

I am in the habit of listening carefully and considering what my husband says. He never speaks lightly to me, for our future depends upon his decisions in this land, and I never reply lightly. Now I say, "Is there reason to think Jesus will foster revolution?"

"Who can say?" he exclaims, pushing away his food and throwing his hands up. "I understand nothing about these people! Some say he preaches revolution already; others say he calls only for peace. Does he think he can have both? That would be a trick for Rome to learn!" We speak no more of Jesus now, but I vow to question Lia more closely. The child may prove invaluable.

When I wake the next morning, she is curled on the floor at the end of my couch. Angry that Katera has ignored my order to find the girl a bed, I shake her. "Why are you here? Did Katera not give you a bed?"

She is quick to protect a fellow slave, "Yes, Lady, but she said I am to serve you and be here when you awake."

Intending to speak to Katera later, I recover my temper. "Go tell her that you will bring my breakfast and that enough should be provided for your own meal." Her eyes light at the thought of sharing my meal, and she runs off. I am dressed when she returns, though the desert heat has robbed me of appetite. I want no more than a few fresh figs, but Lia falls on the tray as if starved. I wonder if my maids shared their evening meal with her, and I regret that I failed to order them to do so. As she eats, I say, "I will have you tell me more of Jesus."

I could not have delighted her more. She tries to speak with a stuffed mouth until I correct her, "Finish your food, and then you may speak." Surprised at my delicacy, she makes quick work of the tray. After setting it aside, she has the presence of mind to ask me, "Shall I bathe your hands and feet first, Lady?"

Hiding a smile, I say, "No. Tell me of Jesus. Does he try to turn the people against Rome? Against Herod?"

She is astonished. "But, Lady, Jesus is not against anyone. He has no ill will for Herod or Rome. The Baptist said that Jesus moves the people to love each other and even love their enemies. This is a new thing in Israel, to love and forgive an enemy! That is why Herod and his woman hate and fear Jesus so much. He brings the Jews a new way of thinking, a way of hope and love, a way to make their way back to the Father. John they could silence, but Jesus will not fall into their trap. Kings and kingdoms of the world mean nothing to him! Once the Herodians and the Pharisees tried to trap him into speaking against Rome. When they asked him publicly if we should pay taxes to Rome, he answered by displaying a denarius and asking, 'Whose head is this and whose title?' When they answered that it was Caesar's, he said, 'Give therefore to the emperor the things that are the emperor's, and to God the things that are God's.' Now tell me, Lady, how could such a man be a threat to Rome?"

How indeed, I wonder.

Lia has been with me for a time now, and she tells me more of Jesus each day. One day I learn from my husband that the leaders are increasingly disturbed about Jesus. "They tell me that he is a problem for Rome and that it is my responsibility to silence him!" Pontius says in frustration. "They seem unable to stop him on their own."

Without stopping to think, I respond, "He is no problem for Rome! Nor was his cousin, John, called the Baptist, whom Herod murdered. These men are not Zealots. Jesus merely annoys the leaders because he preaches a new way. This preaching has nothing to do with Rome, and you should leave it alone." When my husband looks at me questioningly, I add in a subdued voice, "The Hebrew slave from Herod's court has told me of Jesus, his teachings and miracles."

Pontius is not pleased. "And we are to make strategy based on a Jewish slave girl? Be careful! Avoid their interminable religious bickering. Even if this Jesus is no threat to Rome, he will become one if he continues to weaken the Pharisees. Without their rule, I will have no order whatsoever in this desperate land!"

I say no more, but the next day when Lia comes in, she is beside herself with excitement. "Jesus is in Jerusalem," she cries, without even bothering to serve my breakfast. "He is walking and teaching in the Temple region. Lady, let us go and see him!"

The automatic dismissal dies on my lips. Why not? Pontius need not know. I can only do my husband good by learning more about this man and his effect on the people. Lia can see by my face that I am softening, and she leaps at the opportunity, "I will find you clothes to keep you hidden. You must not wear your fine Roman apparel in the Temple or you will be recognized." Before I can caution her or change my mind, she is gone. When she returns, her arms filled with a coarse, hooded robe. When she drapes it over me, I nearly balk. The material is hot and scratchy, and I can barely breathe in its confines. But Lia's eyes are shining as she eagerly takes my hand. Carefully avoiding the household slaves, we slip out.

Soaked with sweat and irritable when we reach the Temple, I soon forget my discomfort. Lia seems to know precisely where Jesus is, and she leads me to where he stands with his disciples, regarding a blind beggar. Concealed behind a massive Temple pillar, we hear a disciple ask, "Rabbi, who sinned, this man or his parents, that he was born blind?" For the first time, I hear the extraordinary voice that has mesmerized thousands. Jesus answers, "Neither this man nor his parents sinned; he was born blind so that God's works might be revealed in him. I must work the works of him who sent me while it is day; night is coming when no one can work. As long as I am in the world, I am the light of the world."

Though his voice is resonant, the words confused me. Yet Lia tightens her grip on my hand, seeming to anticipate what will come next. Without another word, Jesus goes to the blind man, who seems shy at this sudden attention. Jesus spits on the ground, makes mud, and spreads it on the man's eyes. I recoil, but Lia cannot contain her excitement. Jesus raises the man to his feet and tells him to go and wash. When the man stumbles away, I am ready to leave as well. But Lia will not move, whispering urgently, "Only wait, Lady, only wait!" Planning to beat her later for this obstinacy, I prepare to leave without her when the man returns. He strides confidently, his head upright, his arms at his sides. He does not feel about for the way.

He can see.

Moments pass before I can tear my eyes away from this impossible sight, and when I finally do, Jesus is gone. And abruptly, Lia and I reverse our roles. I am determined to find Jesus, but Lia is now afraid for me and demands that we return. When I protest, she insists stubbornly as she pulls me out of the Temple, "We will not find Jesus now, Lady. He has hidden himself. And soon the Temple will be in an uproar. It is our Sabbath, and Jesus has broken the law by healing this day. Soon the priests and Pharisees will swarm all over the Temple, and you could well be discovered."

I am still too stunned by the miracle I have witnessed to resist her, and the part of me that is still the governor's wife knows that I risk trouble if I am seen following Jesus. With a profound disappointment unlike any I have experienced, I reluctantly allow myself to be led back to our quarters. I take to my bed, unable to forget either Jesus' words or the sight of the ecstatic man who could now see.

I do not go in to dinner, and Pontius seeks me out. "Are you ill?" he asks with the gruff concern that makes our match more than a political contract. I look at him and think: he is my husband. I must trust him. When I take his warm hands, he notices my hands are cold and becomes more concerned and starts to massage my fingers. I tell him everything. At first he is infuriated, but his anxiety for my state and his interest in what I had seen gradually overcomes his anger. We talk long into the night, but the situation is now more complicated for him. A host of the Pharisees are demanding he help them stop Jesus, and though he is inclined to do so, my words have given him pause. Because he has not seen what I saw, he views Jesus as a problem of governance.

I tell him, "Whatever the word Messiah means to these people, I know that he is the one." Pontius blanches as if I struck him. Removing his hands gently from my grip, he brushes the damp curls from my face and says, "Guard your heart and words, my wife. If this man becomes a threat to Rome, I must act."

Weeks pass. Jesus is all that anyone talks of. Even my own women are drawn by Lia's stories. She wins their affection, if not their respect, with her lively ways. My husband hardly sleeps anymore. We both lie awake thinking our different thoughts. One night, during the darkest hour, Pontius is called from my chamber. As he leaves he turns to me, his face pale and drawn. "Jesus has been taken," he tells me softly. "And they will surely bring him to me."

I think I will never be able to sleep again, and I rise to pace the length of the room. I am about to call for Lia, when an unnatural, leaden weariness overcomes me, dragging me down until I collapse on my couch. I am suddenly in a room filled with Jewish children, girls and boys, who look worn and starved. They are dressed in rags, and their faces are bereft of joy or life. Lia is among them. Jesus enters the room; he is covered with blood and dirt, his hair tangled with clotted blood, his robe torn, his cloak missing. I want to flee from him, but I cannot abandon Lia. As I push my way into the midst of the children to pull her out to be with me, I see that the children do not fear Jesus as I do. As he approaches, they run to him, their dead eyes now alive with hope and joy. Lia hesitates, and then throws her arms around me for just a moment before she releases me. She goes to Jesus, who takes her into his arms. With the rest of the children, they begin to leave the room, but at the threshold, Jesus and Lia turn toward me. Lia beckons me, "Come, Lady! Come with us!" My heart races at her invitation. I look at Jesus. I was wrong about the blood and filth. It is all disappearing, and before my eyes, Jesus becomes luminescent, almost blinding to look upon, and Lia with him. He smiles at me, and I struggle to move forward, to go with them. But I cannot! I am desperate to escape, to make my feet move, but nothing happens no matter how hard I try. Tears unlike any I ever cried pour from my eyes as Jesus and Lia disappear. I wail in grief.

When I awake, it is to my own scream.

Without waiting even to wash my face, I call for my husband's servant and learn that Pontius is sitting on the judgment seat. Jesus is before him. Trembling violently, I give the slave a message and bid him bring it directly to my husband, "Tell him: 'Have nothing to do with that innocent man, for today I have suffered a great deal because of a dream about him.'"

When he goes I close my eyes, breathing shallowly. After a while, I feel Lia's small, dry hand slip into mine.

Active Meditation

Pilate's wife was affected by the strange new culture in which she found herself. Are you open to learning from other cultures and belief systems? Do you make your beliefs and culture accessible to others? Invite a friend, colleague, neighbor, or family member to a celebration of your faith. It might be a Christmas or Easter service, Sunday Mass, a concert of sacred music, Bible discussion, wedding, funeral or memorial service, or study program. In the same spirit, seek to experience another religion's traditions. Attend a Passover Seder meal, prayer service, gospel music performance, or interfaith community program. You might also read portions of the Torah or the Quran. Even fiction and nonfiction books that focus on other faiths and cultures are helpful. Keep an open mind, and note the many aspects of faith that are shared across religious lines.

Reflection/Discussion Questions

1. Do you think it is better if people of different religions celebrate traditions and beliefs they hold in common or celebrate traditions and beliefs that separate them from one another? Or are both beneficial? Explain your answer.

2. Pilate's wife becomes interested in Jesus through a slave. Give examples from your life when you drew closer to God through others.

3. How do think Pontius Pilate felt when he received his wife's message? What might he have thought as he sat in judgment of another?

CHAPTER XII

Mary Magdalene

Prophet of the Resurrection

LUKE 8:2 AND JOHN 19:25–27; 20:1–18

As I walk in the chilled darkness, I wonder how dawn will ever again stretch its blush across the eastern sky. For me, it is of no matter. All is darkness whether the world calls the time day or night. No sunrise will move me with joy for the day to come, no sunset will bring me hope for tomorrow. In my thirty-five years, I really only lived the past two, and now that life is over.

As the morning dew soaks my sandals on this fateful walk, I consider my life three years ago. I could have never made this journey, even if my purpose had been happier. In those days I never left my house, much less my property. I couldn't. From my tenth year on I was plagued with illnesses of the body, the spirit, and the mind. For over twenty years, I was a prisoner of the malevolent diseases that trapped me. I became a prisoner of my family, of my home.

I was born late in my parents' lives, and my mother was weary of me by the time of my birth. So weary, my father told me, that she decided to die the day after giving me life. My father never forgave me, though I was his only child. My mother had been eager to remove the stain of childlessness from herself and her marriage. Mariam, the woman who kept my father's house, often told me that my mother had desperately wanted me and that, despite her advanced age and thirty years of marriage, my mother had been as excited as a young wife when she learned she was pregnant. That she had died, Mariam assured me throughout my lonely childhood, was not my fault.

My father did not agree. He had as little to do with me as possible, and what attention I do remember receiving from my father when I was a girl was cold dismissal and unrelenting rejection. He left my entire upbringing to Mariam and other servants, and it was with them that I took my meals, learned Scripture, and even slept. Mariam was the only source of love for me, and even her affection was hurried and distracted because she supervised the others who worked to keep my father's property running efficiently. His land was planted with vineyards, and Mariam was the only one he trusted to oversee the workers and wine-makers. Though her intentions toward me were the best, my father saw that she had little time for me. I have since wondered if the lack of time I had with Mariam was just another form of punishment.

I started acting strangely right after my tenth birthday or so, Mariam tells me. I do not recall many details of those early days. Desperation had not yet set in, and I still was not in the habit of keeping a log of my maladies. Mariam told me that it started when I refused to go to bed. I was afraid suddenly, she said, of the dark and of sleep. I complained of horrid nightmares, but I can remember none of them. My earliest memory of my illness is of waking in my pallet in the servant's quarters shrieking because of whatever I dreamed. From the age of ten, I refused to sleep by myself. I insisted on sleeping with Mariam or with one of the other women who served in the house. It was the only way I would ever close my eyes and rest.

When my father ordered Mariam to force me to sleep in my own place, I took a carving knife and slashed my pallet to shreds, or so Mariam told me. I have no memory of it. My father eventually withdrew from the minimal contact I had with him on feast days or Sabbaths. I didn't care. From my childish perspective, he had left me nothing to lose, so I had no reason to try to please him.

Even when I was allowed to sleep with Mariam, I seldom let myself fall asleep easily. As soon as I would begin to fall into a slumber, flashing lights would play upon my eyelids, and I could hear screeching as if the nightmare was calling me. I never knew what would be in the dream. I never remembered the details, just the terror.

Other problems soon followed. Night was not enough for my devouring illnesses, and gradually my days became a maze of fear, pain, and delusion. I saw terrifying-looking creatures peering out from the tangle of grapevines, although I was repeatedly reassured that there was nothing there. I would be talking with a servant and abruptly the features of her face would seem to melt together in a horrible mask of mocking laughter, although her expression had not really changed at all. I saw wolves roaming through the hallways and gardens of our estate, but when I called for help my father's men saw nothing.

Eventually I stopped trusting myself. I never knew what was real and what was a product of my sicknesses. I dared not report what I saw and heard because I knew no one would believe me. By the time I was twelve, everyone except Mariam avoided me, fearing the "master's daughter" and her grievous terrors. The worse punishment was that they kept their children away from me, children who were my only playmates as a girl, children I thought would be my companions as I became a woman. Now these friends looked upon me with empty eyes, and sometimes I saw them as creatures plotting to hurt or kill me.

It is not possible to describe the loneliness of my existence. It is not simply that I was alone but that the people I most loved and needed spurned me. They were afraid of me. I struck out at some of them, hitting, spitting, screaming at them. I seldom remembered these incidents afterwards. I dared not trust myself to appeal to them or promise that I would change, because I couldn't. I was too much in the grip of my diseases, and I could do nothing but cower alone. Of course, what was in me was poisonous, and isolation could only do me more harm. It was agony to know that the human contact I needed to be normal would be forever denied me. My most anguished days were when I felt well and had no delusions, for it was on those days, when I could see the sun in the sky, that I most comprehended the abyss in which I lived. And I had no way to climb out.

Mariam was my only comfort. Though she was the target of my pain and delusional rage as often as anyone else was, she never condemned me. Indeed, she was always ready with forgiveness even when I myself was appalled by my behavior and thought myself unworthy of forgiveness. She seemed to think there was a reason for my sicknesses, no matter how unreasonable they seemed to everyone else, including me. What she told my father of all this, I cannot say. At one point he moved away to his brother's and no longer lived on our estate. I think Mariam must have protected me because he would have taken drastic action against me if he had any regular evidence of my behavior. More than once I heard her warning another servant against sending word to "the master."

I remember overhearing a woman who worked in the fields telling Mariam that if Mariam did not send word to my father, she would. I had thrown a rock at the woman's young son, thinking he was a snake coiled to attack me. Now the woman was infuriated, demanding that Mariam tell my father and have me locked away. Nothing, not even my delusions, frightened me as much as this prospect. At least on our estate, I could wander among the gardens and vineyards and the great hallways of our house. I could breathe the air, take in the scent of the grapes, and pick oranges from the trees. If these small freedoms were taken from me, I would die. If they were taken from me, I would be happy to die. It was that simple. Mariam, usually the soul of kindness and patience, turned on the woman with a vengeance.

"You dare to challenge my judgment? You, who depend upon me for the keeping and feeding of your constantly growing family? You, with a husband who works on this estate as well and depends on this girl's father for his living? You, who owe everything you have to this family? Do you see this girl? Do you see how tortured she is every day? Do you see how her illnesses consume her and bring her more misery than any of us can even begin to understand? Now, look at your children and at the boy whom you claim was so wounded by a glancing blow from a pebble. Are they healthy? Are they able to finish their meals without rising from the table because they think the food is poisoned? Are they able to sleep through the night and wake filled with energy? Are they able to tell the difference between a snake and a boy? A shepherd and a wolf? Are you able to hold them in your arms without them pulling away because your very touch seems to hurt them? Are they able to joke and play with other children without those playmates turning on them with fear and contempt? Will they grow and be able to support themselves and have their own families?"

By the time Mariam finished with her, the woman had crept away, whimpering. But I did not feel vindicated, only ashamed of the litany of my sins and sorrows. I could not begin to imagine how or why Mariam remained my advocate. I could not bring myself to think of what would become of me without her. My constant blessing is that she never left me, even when circumstances all but demanded that she should.

By the time I was twenty, the sicknesses of my body became as powerful as the sicknesses of my spirit and mind. Whether one caused the other, as Mariam believed, I cannot say. Perhaps it does not matter. Regardless, eventually blinding pain intensified my delusions, nightmares, obsessions, and violent behavior. My head hurt, hands, and legs trembled. There was such a clenching in my stomach that I could barely keep food down even when my diseased mind allowed me to eat it. I no longer dared to walk out on our property, lest I fall to the ground in a fit that caused me to foam at the mouth, writhe, and lose my sight. Even Mariam could not control the servants when they witnessed this sight, and a few left my father's service because of it. Mariam and I decided that I should remain within the confines of our house and walled gardens.

This was no great sacrifice for me; I was too physically ill to take long walks, and the sharp scents of the countryside were likely to bring on the pains in my head. Mariam, though still strong, healthy, and well able to govern my father's servants, was growing older, and I spent much of my time with her in the house. These were my only times of peace; often she would rub ointment into my cramped, aching muscles or lay damp cool cloths over my feverish brow.

I was twenty-eight when my father died. He had lived the last years of his life with my uncle, his brother, who owned even more extensive lands than my father. My uncle never visited our home, probably because my father had been too ashamed of me to invite him. Nevertheless, I did not know my uncle, and whatever my father had said to him about me, he did not send word of my father's death until they had buried him. Mariam muttered that the least my father could have done was to leave instructions that he be buried on his own land with his wife. But I knew his disgust for me far overshadowed the memory of my mother; he would not want to be buried near me. These were my thoughts as I considered my father's death from the depths of my abyss.

My father's final punishment came within months of his death. A messenger from my uncle requested that we leave the property because my home was now his. My father had left no assignment of inheritance, and in the absence of such a document, my uncle claimed he was entitled to what he called his "family land." He intended to merge my father's business with his, though what was to become of Mariam and me, his message did not say. Mariam was as furious as I was terrified. While I tried to avoid thoughts about what it would be like to be put out in my current state, Mariam plotted against my uncle. "He has no right!" she fumed. "God told Moses long ago that daughters have the right to inherit when there are no sons, even when there are uncles! He cannot take this land from you. We will bring it before the rabbis and judges. We will prevail."

I didn't have the heart to remind her that when Moses gave God's judgment to those daughters who sought to inherit, he also ruled that they must marry within their tribe. And who, within or without our tribe, would ever marry me?

Mariam was my father's choice to run his estate for a good reason. Though my uncle to this day asserts his claim on our land, he does so privately. Immediately upon learning his intentions Mariam threatened to bring the whole case before rabbis and judges in Jerusalem. And when she told my uncle "the whole case," she made it clear that she meant "the whole case," including me, with my many embarrassing maladies and behaviors. She would make certain that the leaders, whose respect and admiration my uncle cherished, would come to know all about me. I was appalled at her plan, which she freely and happily shared with me, but she assured me it would never come to a public airing. She had been right. Though my uncle protested vehemently and never truly surrendered his claim, he made no move against us. He could not bear the humiliation of acknowledging a mad, sick niece. When Mariam had perceived my lingering hurt over her strategy, she asked me firmly, "Mary, can you think of a better way to turn your father's cruelty against him than to use your sicknesses to thwart his plan?"

We said no more of it, and my uncle has been sputtering these seven years.

My health continued to deteriorate, and eventually Mariam dismissed all our servants and lent the land out to tenant farmers. We survived on the rent they paid us, but our lives became increasingly isolated. I often wondered if Mariam felt the same immeasurable loneliness that I felt, but I never saw a sign of resentment or self-pity in her. "I do not suffer as you do," she explained simply when I asked her how she maintained her peace of mind.

But she did suffer. She had now lived longer than most, and the hard work of caring for me was taking its toll. I could not bring myself to think of what would happen if she became ill or died. I wanted to think I would be able to rise out of my chasm and care for her as she cared for me all these years, but I knew I could not trust myself to do so. And that knowledge was perhaps the most devastating revelation of my miserable life.

Though our house had become like a deserted outpost, word did somehow reach us three years ago about a preacher named Jesus whose teachings and healings had galvanized the country. Mariam became obsessed with the stories of his miraculous healings. Since the house was empty of servants, and we certainly had no visitors, she questioned our tenant farmers and their workers for hours about the man. She would return and tell me with great excitement, "Don't you understand, Mary? It is not just that he heals physical sickness, but that he heals diseases of the mind and spirit as well! He can cure the whole person! We must bring him here!"

If I knew how to laugh, I would have. This famous man, who was cheered and honored by the nation, come here? Here, to our desolate, crumbling house where we could barely feed ourselves, much less

entertain someone of his stature? Here, where he would have no audience, no adoring crowds, no learned discourse? I just looked at her as
if finally she, and not me, had lost her mind. But Mariam set her jaw,
and I should have known she would not let the idea go. In the following days she spent a great deal of time among the tenants who were
known to have heard Jesus. After the next Sabbath, she rose before
dawn and dressed for a journey. Fearful of being left alone for even an
hour, I demanded shrilly, "What are you doing?" (I shudder now to
think how I treated this woman who had stayed beside me when all
others were driven away, and yet to this day, she still dismisses my
pleas for forgiveness as though they are unnecessary.)

She answered calmly, "I have business that will keep me away all
day. I prepared your breakfast and left a simple meal for later that
you can manage on your own. I will be back around dusk."

"You won't!" I accused her in panic. "You are leaving me, I know you
are! You have just been waiting for the opportunity, and now you'll
abandon me!" I began wailing, my eyes tightly closed. Imagine my surprise when she slapped me hard across my face. With all that I put her
through, she had never once struck me. That marvelous fact alone
should have astonished me, but I was too stunned by her slap to think
or say anything at all. With my wailing abruptly cut off, she said in the
same calm voice as if she'd never lifted her hand, "You know me, Mary.
I will be back. This is necessary. Wait as peacefully as you can."

But I had no peace that day. Once she was gone with the rising sun,
every moment became interminable. I made no attempt to eat the
breakfast she left and knew I would not touch the afternoon meal. I
curled tighter into myself on my pallet, and kept my wide eyes on
everything around me. In Mariam's absence there was menace everywhere I looked. The ordinary shadows in the room lengthened and
mutated, becoming creatures who reached long fingers out to grasp me
where I lay, paralyzed with fear. The usual sounds of the tenants as they
harvested the fruit sounded to me like sinister whispers of villains plotting to murder me in my bed. As the day wore on, my body was transformed by my delusions: my stomach cramped, my legs and arms
ached with taut muscles, and my head throbbed as flashes of light
passed before my eyes like swords brandished by the creature-shadows.

By the time the sun was setting, I was barely conscious, writhing on the floor, groaning through clenched teeth, my eyes slit to keep the shadows and light from consuming me. I heard the footsteps approaching and knew I would die. Murderous thieves were about to burst in and cut me open. Even when I felt Mariam's cool hands on my face, I could not bring myself to believe that I was in no danger and that she had truly returned. I had just begun to relax when I heard the man's voice.

"How long has she been like this?"

I flinched and tried to roll away from the voice, a strange man in our home! Mariam betrayed me after all. But now she held me to her, lifting me in her arms, offering me to him. How could she? How could she? She leaned forward and kissed my forehead, murmuring, "Please, Mary. Please, my child."

He took me from her and held me in his arms. Against my will, my warped commands, my body went limp at his touch. What was happening? Where was Mariam? He said, "Mary, look at me." Again, seemingly against my wishes, my eyes were released from their darkness, and I looked into his face. I had seen few men's faces, but this one was extraordinary, not in its separate features but in the whole. He was wonderful to look at, and when my eyes focused, I could see that despite his comforting smile, there were tears on his face. Tears. I suddenly knew that the tears were for me, as if this thought sprung into my mind on its own. In his expression was the reflection of all my years of agony and loneliness and pain, the shining knowledge that he knew what it was like to be in the abyss. He would lift me out. Swept up in a wave of inexpressible relief, I closed my eyes gently.

When I woke he was gone, it was morning, and I was whole.

I went that very day to join the women who followed and ministered to him. I have never left them. Mariam joined us whenever we traveled near my father's estate, and often Jesus and some of the disciples stayed at our home. These were the happiest days of my life; I never imagined I could be so happy. Never.

The memory of those days remains with me even now, despite being cold inside and out. I am frozen and desolate as I make my bleak journey on this lifeless dawn. There are no birds in this garden, no flowers raising their faces hopefully toward the east where surely no sun will rise. I carry the spices and oils with which I will anoint his body, covered with lashes from the whip, pierced by nails, gouged by thorns, stabbed by the spear. The oil and spices weigh little but they seem an unbearable burden, dragging me down and slowing my steps. I have not thought how I will roll back the stone sealing the tomb where they laid him, but I am nonetheless determined to anoint his body. I will find a way. It is all I can do for him now.

The first gray light reveals a sight that quickens my heart, though I scarcely know it is still beating. The stone is rolled back from the tomb. I didn't think I could possibly feel worse. For a moment I have the horrible thought that my eyes are deceiving me, that I am again delusional. But I force the thought away. What I see is true. Someone has removed the stone and taken his body. But why?

Without thinking I turn and run to where I know the followers are gathered, hiding from Jesus' enemies, fearful for their lives. I burst in, crying, "They have taken the Lord out of the tomb, and we do not know where they have laid him!" Many in the group are still sleeping, and when I wake them this way, several look up at me with annoyance, a few with pity. I realize with a flush of shame that they believe what I first feared, that I have again lost my senses, that my illnesses have returned. I want to shout in frustration, but know that will just prove what they already believe. But Peter and John are not asleep, and they look at one another after I speak. Without a word, they start toward the tomb, running; I follow them and am grateful that they believe me. When we reach the tomb, I am relieved to see that the stone is still gone; I am not mad.

But John and Peter are shocked, uncertain what to do. They leave me there, ignoring my pleas that we must find who took Jesus' body. I remain for some time at the tomb, weeping, as the sun slowly rises. When the light comes, I take a deep breath and bend to look in the tomb. Suddenly I cannot breathe. There are two angels sitting there! Why did Peter and John not see them? What is happening to me? Before I can flee, they ask, "Woman, why are you weeping?"

It takes all my courage to answer, "They have taken away my Lord, and I do not know where they have laid him."

The angels make no answer but nod toward something behind me. I turn and see a man, obscured by the vines and trees in this lonely, overgrown place. The one who took the body? Or is he just the gardener? He does not come toward me, but from the screen of leaves asks, "Woman, why are you weeping. Whom are you looking for?"

I beg him, "Sir, if you have carried him away, tell me where you have laid him, and I will take him away."

The man moves forward into the new sunlight and says, "Mary!"

A strangled cry comes forth from me, and I throw myself into Jesus' arms. "Rabbouni!"

After a moment of holding me as he did in that twilight nearly three years ago, he gently releases himself from my fierce embrace and tells me calmly, "Do not hold on to me, because I have not yet ascended to the Father. But go to my brothers and say to them, 'I am ascending to my Father and your Father, to my God and your God.'"

Though I am reluctant to leave him, he is insistent, assuring me I will see him again. I return to the disciples. When I tell them what I have seen and heard, a few still look strangely at me, but I no longer care. They will soon know the truth. I smile kindly at them, knowing that for a second time in my life, I have been made whole and given new life.

Active Meditation

It is easy to understand why Mary was at such a terrible loss after Jesus was crucified. All her hope, her life itself, was based on Jesus. He had given her life, and then he died. You know what Mary did not know in those dark pre-dawn hours: that Jesus had risen! Knowing what you know, do you put all your hope in Jesus? When you consider the "sicknesses" in your life—physical, mental, or spiritual that take a variety of forms including anxiety, ulcers, addictions, pain, and sleeplessness—do you put your hope in Jesus? Do you consider Jesus as the ultimate healer, or do you scratch and scrabble for your own cures and solutions? Make a conscious effort to turn to Jesus. Talk to him. Tell him what is wrong. Ask him to take the burden of illness from you, starting with your false belief that you can do anything without him.

When your burden eases, continue your conversation with Jesus, making certain to express your gratitude. Ask him for the grace to continue to put your hope in him.

Reflection/Discussion Questions

1. The relationship of Mariam and Mary required a great deal of trust and patience. If you have been either a parent or a caregiver, describe the challenges you faced in that capacity. In what way was prayer or spiritual reflection part of the day-to-day relationship?

2. With which of Jesus' cures are you the most comfortable—the cures of physical illnesses like blindness, deafness, or lameness, or the cures of mental and spiritual illnesses during which Jesus drove out unclean spirits? Explain your response.

3. As Mary identified Jesus in the garden, in what ways have you recognized Jesus in others? Although we should always see Jesus in others, were there particular signs that the person you encountered manifested to facilitate Jesus' presence?